Land Rover since 1983

Land Rover since 1983

Coil-Sprung Models

A collector's guide
by James Taylor

MOTOR RACING PUBLICATIONS LTD
Unit 6, The Pilton Estate, 46 Pitlake, Croydon CR0 3RY, England

First published 1996

British Library Cataloguing in Publication Data

Taylor, James, 1950-
    Land Rover since 1983 : a collector's guide : coil-sprung models
    1. Land Rover truck 2. Land Rover truck – History 3. Land
    Rover truck – Collectors and collecting
    I. Title
    629.2'222

ISBN 1-899870-06-7

Printed in Great Britain by
The Amadeus Press Ltd
Huddersfield, West Yorkshire

Contents

Introduction and acknowledgements

MRP published my first *Land Rover Collector's Guide* back in 1984, and four years later asked for it to be updated because so much had happened in the Land Rover world. Since then, Land Rover has gone from strength to strength, and the story of the utility models' development has become more and more fascinating as they have evolved to meet market demands. So when it came to update my *Collector's Guide* yet again, there was really only one way to do it. We have split the book into two volumes, this one dealing with the coil-sprung models which were introduced in 1983 and its forthcoming companion volume dealing with the earlier leaf-sprung models.

In the first 30 years of the Land Rover's history, the vehicles were always closely related to the Rover cars which were built in the same factory complex at Solihull in the West Midlands and with which they shared major engineering components. However, things had changed quite dramatically by the time the Land Rovers covered in this book went on sale, and a deep division had opened up between the car and four-wheel-drive sides of the old Rover company.

Under British Leyland, the car side of the company had been amalgamated first with Triumph in the early Seventies, and then in the early Eighties with the rump of the old Austin-Morris division, itself descended from BMC. What was known by 1983 as Austin-Rover had committed itself to an alliance with the Japanese Honda company which would finally sever all recognizable links with the old Rover Company – and, of course, with the Land Rovers it had built.

In the meantime, Land Rover Ltd had been established as a separate business unit within British Leyland during 1978. During 1982, it had taken over the whole of the Solihull site as car production was moved elsewhere, and the scene was set for a period in which Land Rovers would exist almost independently of Rover cars. That situation lasted until 1989, when the sale of Rover Group (as BL had become) to British Aerospace was folowed by a reintegration of the Rover and Land Rover engineering departments. That would have important consequences for future products, but the Land Rover utitlities – by then renamed Defenders – maintained the independence they had enjoyed since their 1983 introduction. Even the purchase of the Rover Group by the German BMW company in 1994 did not alter them. Despite the age of their basic design, they went on to enjoy an astonishing revival of popularity in the mid-Nineties, and seemed destined to remain in production for many more years both at home and abroad.

Many people gave me a lot of help in putting the present volume together, and I really am grateful for their interest in the project. Alphabetically, then, my sincere thanks go to the Australian Army Technology and Engineering Agency, John Bilton, Mike Broadhead, Patrick Brown, Tony Cope, Robin Craig, the Dunsfold Land Rover Trust, Richard Giller of the Safari Centre in Bryanston (Johannesburg), Mark Griffiths at the Land Rover Centre in Huddersfield, Steven Heath, Peter Hobson of the Land Rover Directory, Land Rover Ltd, Land Rover of North America, *Land Rover Owner* magazine, the Metropolitan Police, Bill Morris, Bob Morrison, Tony Poole, Dave Shephard, Short Bros., and Vantagefield Ltd.

Woodcote, Oxfordshire, April 1996   JAMES L TAYLOR

The Station Wagon version of the Series III, 88in, leaf-sprung, Land Rover in the mid-Sixties.

CHAPTER 1

In the beginning

Developing the coil-sprung Land Rover

By the time the first coil-sprung models went on sale in 1983, Land Rover as a marque had existed for 35 years. Throughout those three and a half decades, its utility models had relied on the same suspension principles of beam axles located and sprung by semi-elliptic leaf springs, and Land Rover engineering chief Tom Barton and his colleagues at Rover's Solihull factory had stuck to their belief that a more comfortable suspension would actually present a threat to the vehicle's longevity. With its traditional cart springs, a Land Rover made its driver acutely uncomfortable long before he had pushed his vehicle to the point where he was likely to damage it!

However, much changed at Solihull in the 15 years leading up to the One Ten's introduction in 1983. A series of mergers during the Sixties saw the old Rover Company absorbed into the British Leyland combine, and in 1978 its Land Rover division was established as a separate operating company. Meanwhile – and perhaps much more important – the huge success of the Range Rover after its 1970 introduction showed that coil springs could be made to work on an all-terrain vehicle. They had been fitted to that vehicle after its designer, Spen King, had been impressed by the rough-terrain performance of a coil-sprung Rover 2000 saloon.

The Land Rovers which immediately preceded the coil-sprung models of the Eighties were the Series III models, available in short-wheelbase 88-inch and long-wheelbase 109-inch forms, and they had progressed hardly at all from the Series IIA models they had replaced in 1971. In a sense,

they were the victims of their ancestors' success. Rover's British Leyland masters were far too concerned with shoring up the ailing car side of their business to worry about new Land Rovers. Their short-sighted view was that the Land Rover was selling well enough as it was, and that there was therefore no sense in investing money in improvements. Besides, the Rover 4x4s had just been supported by the big investment needed to get the Range Rover into production during 1970. If there was any spare money, the Land Rovers were therefore a very long way down the priorities list.

While Land Rover sales held up in the Seventies, the British Leyland view seemed to be justified. Yet as early as 1975, when the British Government asked its chief industrial adviser Sir Don (later Lord) Ryder to look into the affairs of British Leyland, investment in the Solihull four-wheel drives was identified as a high priority. That investment was not made until 1978, at the same time as Land Rover was separated from the Rover Company and made into a self-contained business unit – and by then, it was already too late.

In the Seventies, the Japanese motor manufacturers followed up their successes in exporting cars by designing four-wheel-drive vehicles specifically aimed at Land Rover's traditional overseas markets. A combination of aggressive pricing and better service support than Land Rover could provide made them extremely successful, and in the early Eighties Land Rover saw its markets collapsing dramatically. By 1983 – the year when the new coil-sprung

The vehicles which the new coil-sprung models had to replace were the long-established leaf-sprung Series III Land Rovers, like this 109 Station Wagon.

models were announced – Land Rover was already a spent force in Africa and in many other developing countries which had taken huge quantities of vehicles in earlier years. Economic changes in those countries also left no opportunity for Land Rover to reverse the situation in the short term.

The new Land Rovers therefore had an extraordinarily tough time ahead of them, and it says a great deal for the vehicles themselves and for the company which produced them that they came through the Eighties with flying colours and with the Land Rover reputation not only intact but actually enhanced.

Abortive projects
The Land Rover engineers continued to look at options for new models during the first part of the Seventies, even though the company was being starved of cash and they

were not optimistic that their schemes would ever see the light of day. Their primary objectives were to address the main failings of the current production Series III models, which were their lack of refinement and poor road performance. So different construction methods, improved suspensions, and the Range Rovers' V8 petrol engine all figured in the two major projects for a new Land Rover which occupied Solihull's time between 1972 and 1977.

The first project was for a vehicle called the Series IV Land Rover, and it lasted from 1972 to around 1975. The Series IV might have had some quite revolutionary features, such as an integral 'punt'-type body structure, and it would certainly have had a V8 engine among its optional power units. But most important for the evolution of ideas which resulted in the coil-sprung Land Rovers was its designers' determination to improve the comfort of its suspension. To this end, they planned to use taper-leaf springs, which were

10

The first project for a Land Rover with coil springs was the SD5, although it had them on the front axle only. This full-size styling mock-up was pictured in September 1975, but the project did not survive for very much longer.

already signed-off for the military 101 Forward Control vehicle and would eventually also be taken up by Land Rover's Spanish licencees, Santana. These springs, which had just two leaves, were relatively expensive, but they saved a great deal of weight over the current production multi-leaf springs, and provided a much more compliant ride.

By 1975, the Series IV project had foundered, but the Land Rover engineers carried some of its ideas over to a new project which bore the codename of SD5. (SD stood for Specialist Division, into which British Leyland grouped Rover, Land Rover, Triumph and Jaguar; SD1 was the big new Rover hatchback which was announced in 1976.) Much of the thinking behind this was devoted to simplifying the body structure so that a minimum number of basic body units would produce a large variety of different Land Rovers. However, for SD5 Solihull's engineers also expected to combine traditional semi-elliptic leaf springs at the rear with coil springs on the front axle.

The SD5 project also came to nothing, but it represented

yet another evolution in Land Rover's thinking about better suspensions. As former Land Rover Engineering Director Mike Broadhead recalls, "by 1977 the climate was evidently right for the quite brave decision to accept the cost of coils all round."

A hybrid prototype

In fact, the very first Land Rover with all-round coil springs had already been built by the time the new project got under way. It was more concept vehicle than prototype, having been constructed during 1976, apparently in response to an idea from Land Rover's product planners to create a sports-utility vehicle for the American market. Legend has it that there was no budget to build a concept vehicle, and so someone arranged for the Land Rover apprentices to build one as an exercise! John Bilton, a product planner at the time, remembers the concept being known as a Land Rover 100-inch Station Wagon, which must have caused some confusion because that same name had been given to the Range Rover when it was under

development some 10 years earlier.

The vehicle was a fascinating hybrid. It was built on a Range Rover chassis, with a Land Rover rear crossmember and outriggers welded to it. Its body came from a Series III 109-inch Station Wagon, but was shortened behind the rear axle and cobbled together with wooden battens where areas of its steel frame had to be cut away. To accommodate the Range Rover axles – five inches wider than Series III Land Rover items – the wheelarches were crudely enlarged with tin snips. The metal roof of the Station Wagon and the rear body sides behind the doors were replaced by a purpose-built soft-top, and a reinforcing bar behind the front seats replaced the lost rigidity. Grille, bonnet and windscreen were all individually-built items (though all closely anticipated later production Land Rover parts). The engine and transmission were both Range Rover items, being a 130bhp 3,528cc petrol V8 and a four-speed permanent four-wheel drive system respectively. Among the vehicle's more fascinating features were striped bucket seats from an MGB sportscar both front and rear, giving a strictly four-

seat configuration with considerably more comfort than any production Land Rover of the time could offer. No doubt these were justified as being part of the sports-utility specification intended to suit the US market.

The concept of a sports-utility Land Rover for the USA never did go any further – at least, not until the NAS 90 some 15 years later – but the 100-inch Land Rover did not become redundant. Instead, it was snapped up by the Land Rover engineers when the project for a coil-sprung Land Rover began in earnest, and spent the next few years as an off-road test hack at Land Rover's Eastnor Castle proving ground in Herefordshire. It was never given a serial number and never registered for the road, but it does still exist and is now part of the remarkable collection of rarities owned by the Dunsfold Land Rover Trust.

A two-part strategy

By the beginning of 1977, plans were being formulated for the massive injection of capital into the Solihull four-wheel drives which the Ryder Report had recommended. For the

Land Rover utilities, a two-part strategy was drawn up, the first to improve the existing Series III models and the second to develop a completely new range of vehicles.

In the short term, the existing Series III models would get a much-needed power boost from the installation of the V8 petrol engine, which would bring with it the Range Rover's permanent four-wheel-drive transmission. This would be funded under Stage 1 of the planned investment scheme, and indeed these models would always be known as the Stage 1 V8 Land Rovers as a result. They would be announced in 1979, and the following year would see revitalized four-cylinder engines, with five-bearing crankshafts instead of the existing three-bearing types. Next would come a wider range of bodies in the shape of a High-Capacity Pick-Up on the long-wheelbase chassis and County Station Wagons with upgraded trim and equipment levels. Only after these had been introduced – which actually happened in April 1982 – would it be time to announce the all-new models developed under the long-term strategy.

The funding for the long-term strategy was allocated under Stage 2 of the Land Rover investment plan, and so the all-new models were known as Stage 2 Land Rovers right from the start. Work on them went ahead in parallel with the development work to support the short-term strategy. Project Notes prepared in April 1977 by Mike Broadhead, who was then Assistant Chief Engineer to Tom Barton, show that the focus in the beginning was on two different wheelbases – the 100-inch of the existing Range Rover and a 110-inch which was intended to replace the Series III 109-inch models.

Exactly why the 110-inch wheelbase had been chosen is not clear, although it was fairly obvious that a wheelbase of around this size would have been necessary to replace the existing 109-inch Land Rovers. However, it might not have been entirely coincidental that a 110-inch coil-sprung chassis already existed, in the shape of the long-wheelbase Range Rover chassis developed for ambulance conversions by Spencer Abbott. To create an initial feasibility prototype, one of these was fitted during 1978 with the body of a 109-inch Land Rover. A little adjustment was needed in the

Even before the Stage 2 project officially existed, the Land Rover stylists had been looking at ways of adapting wide-track axles to the existing body panels. This mock-up dates from 1976, and shows metal 'eyebrows' and an experimental bumper style on wide-track axles which are still on leaf springs.

middle of the body and behind the rear axle, but the result was the very first One Ten V8 – another vehicle which now belongs to the Dunsfold Land Rover Trust's remarkable collection.

During 1977, Bob Lees was appointed as Project Engineer to co-ordinate the work of all the different engineering departments involved with the Stage 2 Land Rovers, and for the next four years, development of the 100-inch and 110-inch models went ahead in parallel. After the first Range Rover-based prototypes had been tested, the chassis frames of both variants were reinforced with deeper sidemembers, drawn up by Trevor Greenway of the chassis section, with the result that the frames ended up looking very different from the original Range Rover types. A decision was also taken to use drum brakes on the rear axle

It was the Styling Department's job to look at colour schemes for the Stage 2 models. This One Ten High-Capacity Pick-Up was painted in an attractive two-tone colour scheme which was not adopted for production. It was pictured at a colour review session, when Land Rover's Managing Director, Mike Hodgkinson, and other senior managers in the company were checking on progress.

instead of the disc brakes fitted to the Range Rover, and to use the Range Rover's self-levelling rear suspension only on the passenger-carrying Station Wagon variants of the Stage 2 Land Rover. The primary reason for these changes was, of course, to minimize the production cost of the new vehicle and thus to hold its price to the customer at levels which would be competitive with the Land Rover's rivals.

While the Stage 2 Land Rover chassis evolved away from that of its Range Rover parent, other Range Rover features remained unchanged. The vehicle's wider track brought with it valuable additional stability (although the axles themselves were developed further to withstand heavy-duty use), and its permanent four-wheel drive system offered so many benefits for on-road handling and traction that it also remained in the Stage 2 specification. In addition, splitting the driving torque evenly between two axles avoided the need for a rear axle capable of taking all the torque of the V8 engine. Such a heavy-duty axle would have added to the development and manufacturing costs of the new vehicle,

and its weight would have worked against the ride refinement which the coil-spring suspension brought with it.

Even though the V8 engine was central to the Stage 2 project, it would certainly not be the only power unit on offer. Completely new engines were ruled out on cost grounds for the time being, and so Land Rover planned to supplement the V8 with modernized versions of the elderly four-cylinder petrol and diesel types then available in the Series III models. The V8, too, would be uprated from its Stage 1 tune, and for the Stage 2 vehicle it would be 25% more powerful and offer a similar amount of extra torque.

Cost restrictions prevented the Land Rover engineers from doing very much with the 2,286cc indirect-injection diesel engine, however. In fact, it retained its Series III specification, with 62bhp at 4,000rpm and 103lb.ft of torque at 1,500rpm. For improvements, it had to make do with nothing more than a key-operated (solenoid) cut-out instead of the cable-operated cut-out of the Series III and

earlier models. Nevertheless, there would be some real improvements for the four-cylinder petrol engine, which shared its 2,286cc capacity, five-bearing crankshaft and overhead-valve design with the diesel. For its Stage 2 application, Land Rover resolved to improve its low-speed torque, and to that end the engineers redesigned its inlet and exhaust manifolds, fitted a new camshaft and specified a Weber 32/34 DMTL carburettor in place of the earlier Solex. The results were 74bhp at 4,000rpm and 163lb.ft at 2,000rpm.

It was once again cost which dictated the choice of transmissions for the Stage 2 Land Rovers. Although the Solihull engineers would have liked to offer five-speed gearboxes on all versions of their new vehicle in order to improve fuel economy, the only five-speed gearbox available to them was not strong enough in existing form to cope when installed behind a V8 engine and subjected to rough treatment. For the time being, the V8 Land Rovers would have to have the LT95 four-speed gearbox used in the Range Rover.

The fundamental engineering change on the Stage 2 vehicles was to coil springs, which had proved their superiority over leaf springs on the Range Rover. This is the rear suspension on a One Ten, showing the long-travel coil spring itself, the hefty telescopic damper and the radius arm which helped locate the axle.

Styling Department work in the late Seventies included development of a windscreen which was big enough to meet regulations in all the countries where the new Land Rovers would be sold. As the bulkhead and scuttle ventilator area had to remain unchanged, the windscreen had to be enlarged upwards.

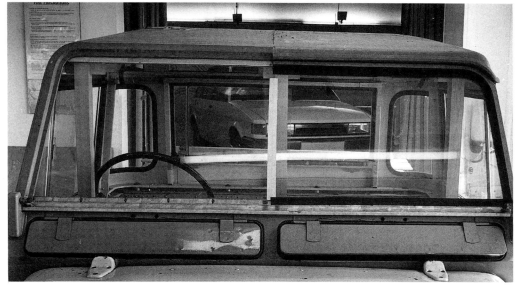

However, the two four-cylinder engines planned for the new Land Rover had much lower torque outputs than the V8. The five-speed LT77 gearbox – introduced for the Rover SD1 saloon and the Triumph TR7 sportscar in the mid-Seventies – could therefore be used behind these without problems. What Land Rover did need was a new transfer box to go with it, and Solihull's transmissions people came up with a new design called the LT230R. This was designed to give permanent four-wheel drive, and had delightfully simple control from a single lever with an H-gate which selected High and Low ranges (to the right) and locked the centre differential in either range (to the left).

Land Rover nevertheless suspected that there would still be some customers who would demand the traditional selectable four-wheel drive, not least because this type of transmission was the only one available in the Land Rover's Japanese competitors. So it was that the four-cylinder models would be made available optionally with the new LT77 five-speed primary gearbox coupled to a special transfer box which offered rear-wheel drive only in High range. In the event, the customers would take to permanent four-wheel drive so wholeheartedly that Land Rover would abandon the selectable option after the Stage 2 models had been on sale for just over a year.

The military 100-inch
While work went ahead on the 100-inch and 110-inch vehicles, Solihull was also running a parallel project to develop a 100-inch military vehicle. The Land Rover military sales people, ever alert to the possibility of a large order, had managed to interest both the French and the Swiss Armies in the possibility of a coil-spring 100-inch Land Rover, and as it was important to have vehicles to show them rather than simply drawings, a number of prototypes were built during 1978.

In fact, neither the French nor the Swiss Army ever made an order. Swiss interest seems to have waned in 1980 or 1981, allegedly when Land Rover were unable to make the engines meet the tough Swiss emissions regulations. The French contract meanwhile went to the Peugeot P4, a version of the Mercedes-Benz G-Wagen built under licence

in France. It looks as if Land Rover next tried to interest the British Army in the 100-inch vehicle in addition to the One Tens, and in fact the 100-inch project was not terminated until 1986. By that time, according to one estimate, around 70 prototypes had been built. Some had V8 petrol engines and some had four-cylinder petrol engines; some had automatic transmissions with limited-slip differentials in the front and rear axles; some had five-door Station Wagon bodies and others had General Service soft-top types. Several of these prototypes still survive, either in museum collections or in private hands.

The Ninety enters the picture
In the meantime, a great deal had happened on the coil-sprung Land Rover project as a whole. During 1980, Tom Barton had retired as Engineering Director, and Mike Broadhead had taken over from him. It must have been shortly after that when the engineers and product planners got together to review progress on the Stage 2 Land Rovers, and one of the main items on the agenda was which wheelbase sizes to use for production.

At this stage, the two under consideration were the 100-inch and 110-inch, but Mike Broadhead was among those who felt that the 100-inch was too big as a replacement for the Series III 88-inch size. So the concept arose of a 90-inch wheelbase for the smaller Stage 2 vehicle, and that won the day. The 100-inch was therefore sidelined as a production model, although work would continue on the military 100-inch Stage 2 vehicle.

However, the wheelbase did not remain at 90 inches for long. After just one prototype had been built in the Experimental Shop during 1981, Mike Broadhead took a long hard look at the vehicle. The adjustable driver's seat which had been a feature of Stage 2 since the beginning inevitably took up quite a lot of space and, of course, took several inches from the rear body length. Anxious to make the new Land Rover better in every way than the 88-inch Series III it was to replace, he decided to restore that lost length, and to add a little more for good measure. The only way to do this was to increase the wheelbase, and so it was that the distance between axle centres went up to 92.9

By 1981, Land Rover had decided that the short-wheelbase Land Rover would have a 90-inch wheelbase. This prototype – now preserved by the Dunsfold Land Rover Trust – was built by cut-and-shut methods in the Experimental Shop, using One Ten parts. However, it was to be the only one with this wheelbase length; subsequent vehicles had a 92.9-inch wheelbase and incorporated various improvements which Engineering Director Mike Broadhead insisted upon.

inches, which makes better sense expressed as 2,360mm in the metric units with which Land Rover was by now working. However, the marketing men found the name Ninety rather more snappy than Ninety-Two Point Nine, and thus the new short-wheelbase model got the name with which it would be announced in 1984.

Styling

Early prototypes were built using existing Series III and Stage 1 V8 production body panels as far as possible, partly because they came readily to hand and partly because they helped to disguise what the vehicles actually were. However, the Land Rover stylists, working under the direction of Tony Poole, had been asked as early as 1978 to give the Stage 2 vehicles a distinctive appearance.

Initial styling work was done on two prototype 100-inch models which were delivered to the studios at Drayton Road. It was established very early on that there should be a one-piece windscreen and that this would have to be deeper than the existing two-piece screen in order to meet regulations about wiped area in some of the vehicle's intended markets. As the bulkhead with its scuttle

ventilators could not be altered, the stylists had to enlarge the screen upwards and above the level of the door windows – a solution with which Tony Poole was never happy. Also established early on was that the widened tracks would be covered by wheelarch 'eyebrows' rather than by a wider body, primarily because of the cost of tooling up for new body panels. In addition, it was clear that there would have to be a flush front end to suit the V8 engine installation, and so to save costs the same panelling was adopted for the four-cylinder variants as well.

By March 1981, these styling ideas had firmed up, and full-sized One Tens submitted for viewing by Managing Director Mike Hodgkinson in July 1982 looked very much like the eventual production vehicles. They did incorporate certain details which were not approved – such as black wheel centres and different two-tone colour splits – but in essence the Styling Department's proposals were accepted unchanged. The body they had come up with was immediately recognizable as a Land Rover, and yet it was a distinctive evolution which in time would become as much loved and respected as the shapes which had gone before.

Prototypes were assembled using as many existing production parts as possible. This metal fillet in the side of the second Ninety prototype compensates for the difference between its 92.9-inch wheelbase and the 88-inch wheelbase of the Series III model for which most of its body panels were intended!

CHAPTER 2

End of an era

One Tens and Ninetys, 1983-85

By the middle of 1982, it was quite clear what Land Rover's new-model strategy would be. The Stage 2 110-inch wheelbase model was the furthest advanced of the three types under development, and this would be introduced to the market first. The 90-inch model, which lagged some way behind in development, would appear a year or so later. As for the intermediate-wheelbase 100-inch, that would remain a military-only project. The two new models would replace the existing Series III types gradually over a period of around two years, partly so that existing fleet orders for the older vehicles could be fulfilled, but also because some markets would take time to adapt to the greater sophistication and – inevitably – greater cost of the new models.

Official word of the forthcoming Land Rover 110 Stage 2, as it was called, went out from the factory during September 1982 in the guise of a confidential descriptive brochure sent to the approved aftermarket converters by the Special Projects department. "In the 110 Land Rover," this read, "we have combined the highly superior on- and off-road ride qualities of the Range Rover with the more practical range of Land Rover body styles to create a totally new vehicle which sets new standards in 4x4 motoring and manufacturing technology. To meet the exacting needs of the individual Land Rover customer a full range of petrol and diesel engines are offered which give increased power over their predecessors.

"All-new five-speed transmissions on four-cylinder derivatives are offered for the first time on Land Rover and indeed for the first time on any 4x4 in its class, which combined with the new simple-to-operate single-lever transfer box and permanent four-wheel drive give excellent on-road performance.

"A new chassis design with long-travel coil springs, front disc brakes with rear drums offers higher payloads and the option of levelled suspension, similar to that of the Range Rover. The front axle datum relative to the Series III Land Rover moves back 2⅛in and the rear 3⅛in, which accounts for the 1in increase in wheelbase. Wheel apertures in the front and rear body move the same distance and incorporate deformable eyebrows to accommodate the wider track. The distance from front axle to rear door pillar on the Station Wagons has not changed.

"Many other detail changes have been made which are designed to provide greater user comfort, eg dash/instrument panel, one-piece windscreen and front grille panel. A wide range of optional extras will be available including in-dash air conditioning, winches, PTO, power steering and trim."

Over the next six months, as the first pre-production vehicles were assembled to test build methods, Land Rover's sales and marketing departments drew up their plans to handle the new vehicle. In addition, they chose a date for its public announcement: March 1983. The real reason for that choice was to give the 110 maximum international exposure at the Geneva Show, but by a clever twist of marketing the launch was also made to commemorate the 35th anniversary of the Land Rover's

The One Ten still looked like a Land Rover, but was a very different animal from earlier types, especially on the road. This picture shows a hardtop of the 1983 launch publicity fleet, with one of the CWK registration numbers associated with those vehicles.

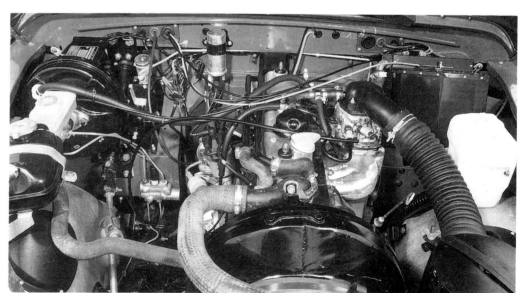

The five-bearing 2.3-litre petrol engine had been slightly uprated from its Series III application and featured a Weber carburettor in place of the earlier Solex.

announcement at the April 1948 Amsterdam Show.

Publicity material for the new vehicle described it as "Land Rover's new Land Rover", and the vehicle wore a plastic badge above its radiator grille which bore the legend 'Land Rover 110'. However, most printed sales and marketing material insisted on the name of Land Rover One Ten, which followed on logically from the long-wheelbase Series III model's accepted name of 'One-O-Nine'. This snappy marketing name also helped to avoid confusion with the Land-Rover 110-inch Forward Control model of the late Sixties and early Seventies and – for those with even longer memories of Solihull's products – with the Rover 110 saloon of 1962-64.

The marketplace, 1983-85

Yet despite the optimism which lies behind all new-model launches, there were some worried faces at Land Rover as the new One Tens came on-stream. The fact was that Land Rover sales had started to collapse in 1980, and by the time of the One Ten's launch in 1983 the future was looking grim. Nor was the situation one which could be salvaged by the new models; the fact was that Land Rover had lost its traditional markets to Japanese competitors and it would take years to win them back.

In fact, it was not the utility models which saw Land Rover through the early Eighties, but rather the Range Rover. Investment in new models at the beginning of the decade paid off, and sales gradually increased, offsetting the catastrophic decline in sales of the Land Rover utilities. In the first few years of the new decade, Land Rover actually lost money for the first time in its entire history, and it was primarily increased Range Rover sales which allowed it to turn in a modest profit of £2 million on a £400 million turnover in 1984. Sales of the utility models, meanwhile, continued to fall.

In the 1981 calendar year, itself some 20% down on 1980, the company had sold 41,059 Land Rovers; for 1982 the figure was 38,926. Despite positive reactions to the new One Ten, sales for 1983 (which included some of the outgoing Series III models) were down to 28,412. The next

Discreet side stripes and a name decal at the rear of the body sides mark this early vehicle out as a County Station Wagon.

year saw a further slip, to 25,663; the 1985 figures were again worse at 23,772; and during 1986 the company hit rock bottom with just 19,195 sales of Land Rovers worldwide.

Solihull's management took a number of steps to bring the company back to greater profitability. In the period between 1978 and 1982, when Mike Hodgkinson was Managing Director at Land Rover, the effort went into product improvement. From 1983, when Tony Gilroy took over, the effort went into streamlining the manufacturing operation and into seeking new markets to replace those which had been lost.

With the One Ten already on sale, Gilroy set about a radical reorganization of the Land Rover manufacturing operation, following the first moves in this direction made under Mike Hodgkinson. Under Hodgkinson, Rover car manufacture had been moved out of the Solihull plant, which had become a dedicated four-wheel-drive manufacturing operation from early in 1982. In November 1983, the streamlining operation was publicly announced. No fewer than nine 'feeder' factories in the Midlands and Wales which made Land Rover components would be closed down over the next two years, and all production and assembly work would be centralized at the Solihull site. The intention – fully realized in practice – was that the streamlining should save the company a substantial £14 million a year when it was completed.

Gilroy also arranged for a thorough review of Land Rover's markets, existing and potential, and on the results of this he based his strategy for the company's future. It would be too costly and risky to try to win back those markets lost to the Japanese, and so Gilroy chose to target continental Europe and the USA, where expectations of the four-wheel-drive vehicle were quite different from expectations in Africa. To compete successfully here would therefore entail a thorough reorientation of existing products and design philosophy. As one part of this dual-pronged strategy, the Range Rover would be developed for the US market; and as the other, the Land Rover utilities would be developed for Europe.

Yet all this was going on behind the scenes. For the period from 1983 to 1985, the coil-sprung Land Rovers and the final leaf-sprung Series IIIs which remained on sale alongside them were engaged in a struggle for survival in their traditional African, Middle Eastern and other Third World markets.

The first One Tens

The new One Ten models were made available only in Britain and Switzerland at first, although they were rapidly introduced to other markets throughout 1983. In Britain, they completely replaced the Series III 109-inch models, although in some territories the two types were briefly on sale together. Availability of the Series III 88-inch models, of course, remained unchanged.

There was a great deal that was new about the One Ten, but there was also a great deal that was comfortingly familiar. Not only was the general outline of the vehicle very similar to that of the Series III 109, but the familiar range of five body types remained available, all panelled in Birmabright aluminium alloy as Land Rovers had been since 1948. The five types were the soft-top, hardtop, pick-up, high-capacity pick-up (HCPU or Hi-Cap) and Station Wagon (available with both basic and de luxe County specifications); the One Ten could also be supplied in chassis/cab form for special bodywork. The choice of three engines was also familiar, despite the improvements made to the four-cylinder and V8 petrol types.

Yet a One Ten was instantly distinguishable from earlier Land Rovers. There were major differences at the front of the vehicle, where the deep single-piece windscreen offered a 25% increase in area as compared with the divided Series III type. Also unmistakable was the new flush front, with its black plastic slatted grille and matching black plastic headlamp surround panels. The heater air intake in the front wing – always on the side opposite to the driver – could now be found on top of the wing instead of in its side, and was matched by a dummy intake on the opposite wing; the neatly shaped bonnet panel, with a shallow depression in its centre, was quite different from what had gone before.

Most obvious from the sides were the deformable eyebrows fitted over the wheelarches, which were designed

By later standards, the dashboard of this early One Ten County looks quite spartan, but it was a big improvement over the crude dashboards of the Series III and earlier vehicles.

to afford a degree of protection to the body sides and to compensate for the widened tracks of the One Ten. They also gave the vehicle a pleasantly rugged appearance, which was very much in keeping with its utility role. At the rear, the tail-lamps were mounted on the lower body corners instead of at waist level as on the Series III. On Station Wagons, customer complaints about the Series III had been met by fitting a third hinge on the rear door and by mounting the exterior spare wheel higher up, to leave room for a tow hitch on the rear crossmember. Lastly, the One Ten came with its own range of paint colours: some were continued from the Series III, but the more garish hues available only on the Stage 1 V8 models were discontinued and the One Ten could be had in three new colours: Roan Brown, Stratos Blue and Trident Green.

By comparison with the spartan Series IIIs, the One Tens were almost luxurious inside even though they retained their workmanlike character. The dashboard was a completely new moulding and the instrument panel ahead of the driver was very much neater and more legible than

the Series III type. A four-spoke steering wheel, similar to that on the Range Rover but with the Land Rover name moulded into its centre pad, replaced the old three-spoke type. Front seats offered a greater range of adjustment than on any previous Land Rover, and the neater appearance of the gear-levers and handbrake was further enhanced by tough rubber gaiters. Overall, the interior of the One Ten seemed much more car-like than that of earlier Land Rovers.

Road behaviour was also more car-like. Earlier Land Rovers with their leaf-spring suspension had given a rough, jolty ride, but the coil-sprung One Tens rode much like a Range Rover. The ride was altogether more forgiving and comfortable, although the long-travel coil springs did allow rather more body roll on corners than the leaf springs had done. In rough terrain, these springs also made the One Ten much more capable than its predecessors, because the increased travel (up by 50% at the front and by 25% at the rear) allowed greater axle articulation, which in turn increased the chances that the wheels would remain in

The coil-sprung Land Rovers were quickly pressed into use by the emergency services. This One Ten Accident Unit had entered service with the Thames Valley Police by 1984.

contact with the ground in extreme conditions. Braking – which could cause some anxious moments in a heavily-laden long-wheelbase Series III – was also transformed by the front discs and vacuum servo.

Reactions to the One Ten

The One Ten was an immediate success. A test drive either on or off the road almost invariably won over existing Land Rover owners, and the new model's considerable virtues gave it an appeal far beyond traditional Land Rover territory. Overseas, the majority of sales were of the utility variants; in Britain, however, for every farmer or construction company which bought a utility model, there appeared to be a family which bought a One Ten instead of a conventional two-wheel-drive estate car. This was the time when the Eighties' boom in passenger-carrying 4x4s was just beginning, and the One Ten's new-found refinement put it in a strong position which Land Rover would later exploit to the hilt.

In such circumstances, it was not surprising that the biggest success belonged to the County Station Wagons. Sales exceeded Land Rover's own expectations, and it was these vehicles which really created the One Ten's image in the home market and would go on to do the same in other developed countries. The County Station Wagons came with a great deal of special equipment, some of it also optionally available on other models, and could be easily recognized by their side-stripe decals and 'County' badges on the sides and rear.

The levels of equipment which came as standard on the One Ten County would have been unthinkable just a few years earlier on a Land Rover. The County specification included tinted glass, brown cloth upholstery, rubber pedal pads, halogen headlamps, front and rear mudflaps, a reversing lamp, a dipping interior mirror, a clock, a voltmeter, an ashtray and sun visors. The headlining was made of resin-impregnated felt, which had good sound-insulating properties and so made it unnecessary to fit the Tropical roof of earlier Station Wagons. There were side repeater flashers on the front wings, a hazard warning system, a spare-wheel cover and a bonnet lock. In addition, there were self-levelling rear suspension, power-assisted steering and radial tyres in place of the crossplies fitted to other models.

As Land Rover customers expected, a wide range of optional equipment was available. This covered both utility equipment, such as winches and power take-offs, and other types of extras. These were available either individually or grouped into option packs covering electrical, protection, towing and interior appointment additions. For more specialist applications, the Special Projects Department at Solihull was busily working with the converters to prepare the familiar array of fire tender, ambulance and other special-bodied derivatives; and the military sales people were quick off the mark with a prototype which they could show to their customers.

The 2.5-litre diesel engine
The One Ten range did not remain unchanged for long. As related in Chapter 5, it was joined towards the end of 1983

by the extended-wheelbase Crew Cab model; and then a few weeks later Land Rover announced an enlarged diesel engine to replace the 2.3-litre type.

This was the second phase of a development programme on the diesel engine which had been initiated in the late Seventies. The results of the first stage had been seen in 1980, when the five-bearing version of the engine was announced; work had started on this second stage almost immediately after that. In an ideal world, Solihull would have had the 2.3-litre engine ready for announcement in the One Ten in 1983, but as usual the company was constrained by limited money and resources. So it was that the more powerful diesel engine was long overdue by the time it was announced at the Amsterdam Show on February 4, 1984.

The engine's new capacity of 2,495cc had been achieved by lengthening its stroke – hardly a revolutionary change and indeed one which had been tried experimentally as long ago as 1962! However, the toothed rubber belt which replaced the roller timing-chains of the 2.3-litre engine *was*

The 1985-season facelift is seen to good effect on this One Ten County. There are neatly rounded corners to all the side windows, and the winding front door windows are all of a piece. The side decals have also changed.

new. This belt also drove the new DPS injector pump which gave more accurate fuel metering, retained its tune for longer than earlier types and minimized fuel consumption. The pump also benefited from a self-priming system instead of the hand primer of earlier types. Cold-weather starting of the new engine was improved by means of more efficient sheathed-element glow-plugs, and the new alloy castings used for its water pump housing and front cover also saved weight.

"There will not be a 2.5-litre petrol engine", insisted Land Rover's own Product Bulletin of December 1983, which advised dealers of the forthcoming new engine. While that statement was true at the time it was made, subsequent events would change the picture completely....

The 1985-model One Tens

The selectable four-wheel drive option on the early four-cylinder One Tens had found few takers, and when the 1985 models were announced in June 1984, permanent four-wheel drive was standardized. The 1985 specification also incorporated a number of changes to equipment levels, which made the vehicles seem less utilitarian than before. Nevertheless, their workhorse ability remained undiminished.

The 1985-model or 'facelifted' One Tens were readily recognizable, even at a distance, by their single-piece front door windows. Earlier models had been fitted with detachable door tops and sliding windows, like their Series III counterparts, but Land Rover had belatedly recognized that these were rather crude devices – particularly for a vehicle of the County Station Wagon's cost and pretensions. So, for the first time on a Land Rover utility, the 1985 models came with winding windows. However, the doors were still made in two pieces to save manufacturing costs, and the join was still concealed by a galvanized garnish rail.

With the new window arrangements came smart moulded interior door trims, incorporating locking buttons on their sills. Station Wagons also had modified sliding windows in the rear, which tidied up their appearance. Soft-tops and three-quarter tilts were now supplied in Matt Stone instead of Khaki, presumably because the new colour had a rather less military appearance; needless to say, Khaki soft-tops were still available for military buyers.

Standard equipment levels had also been increased, and the trend towards greater comfort initiated by the County Station Wagons was now readily visible right across the range. The reason, of course, was that more car-like utility vehicles – particularly from Toyota – had changed customer expectations in this area of the market. So it was that all One Tens sold after June 1984 came with a cigarette lighter, a steering column lock, a bonnet lock, a fuel filler lock and a dipping interior mirror. Station Wagons now came as standard with a heated rear window and rear wash-wipe, both of them very welcome additions.

County Station Wagons continued to head the range. Their list of standard equipment was lengthened slightly by the addition of twin radio speakers and an aerial (the customer had to choose a radio or radio/cassette and pay extra for it), and by the addition of carpeting in the passenger area. There were new side decals, too, this time colour co-ordinated with the main body colour and themselves in two tones with the 'County' name emblazoned across the front doors. To those used to Land Rover's pace of change in earlier times, the annual changes of the Eighties seemed like a revolution – but they were necessary if the company's products were to remain competitive.

The Ninety

Ever since the launch of the One Ten, no-one outside Land Rover had ever doubted that there would eventually be a companion short-wheelbase coil-sprung Land Rover. Solihull would not, of course, make any official comment on the matter, and the rumours which began to circulate as a result certainly heightened the sense of excitement and anticipation which was felt in some parts of the Land Rover world.

The Ninety was eventually launched in June 1984, at the same time as the facelifted 1985-model One Tens. It therefore benefited from all the 1985 specification improvements including, of course, permanent four-wheel

The short-wheelbase companion to the One Ten was finally announced in June 1984 as the Ninety. This County Station Wagon is one of the launch publicity vehicles and wears an appropriate registration number.

drive as standard. However, much to the disappointment of those who took an interest in Land Rover matters, it was not made available with the V8 petrol engine. Instead, customers had to make do with the 2.3-litre four-cylinder petrol and 2.5-litre four-cylinder diesel types.

The Ninety's arrival sounded the death knell for the leaf-sprung Series III models. In Britain and in several other markets, it replaced the 88-inch models immediately, although the older vehicles remained in production for around 12 months longer to meet outstanding fleet orders. During the summer of 1985, however, the assembly lines which had turned out leaf-sprung Land Rovers were converted to build coil-sprung types, and the 88s and 109s disappeared from Solihull altogether.

The Ninety shared its styling cues with the One Ten, and the two were instantly recognizable as brothers, just as the 88 and 109 Series IIIs had been. Like the One Ten, the Ninety, of course, had disc front brakes to complement its coil-spring suspension. The five-speed LT77 gearbox and the LT230R transfer box were standard equipment, although the lighter weights of the short-wheelbase models had enabled the Land Rover engineers to specify a taller and more fuel-efficient 'High' ratio in their transfer boxes than was possible for the One Tens.

Compared with the Series III 88-inch model, the Ninety was 4.4in longer overall and, like the 88, it had a shorter rear overhang than its long-wheelbase brother. This had the advantage of improving the departure angle for rough-

The Ninety quickly found favour with the emergency services, its rugged strength and handiness proving an ideal combination. This example was taken on by HM Coastguard in 1985...

... and this Station Wagon suited the needs of London's Metropolitan Police.

terrain driving, and in addition it placed the wheels almost ideally at each corner of the vehicle to give the best possible ride. Meanwhile, the extra 4.9 inches in the wheelbase as compared with the Series III 88 had allowed Land Rover to provide more cargo space and improved front seat travel.

Payload, too, was increased: by between 14% and 33%, depending on the body type. As with the Series III 88, four different bodies were built on the assembly lines, these being the soft-top, hardtop, pick-up and seven-seater Station Wagon. Station Wagons could be ordered with County trim, and the Ninety was also made available to order as a chassis/cab for special bodywork.

Like the One Ten before it, the Ninety made its mark at once. In the traditional Land Rover workhorse market, its improved carrying capacity was welcomed and its much enhanced ride comfort enabled faster and longer journeys to be made than were possible in any earlier short-wheelbase model. Meanwhile, it also scored well in the growing leisure market, where County Station Wagon variants provided a credible and remarkably civilized alternative to a conventional car-derived estate.

This Ninety hardtop was taken on by the Northamptonshire Police in the mid-Eighties.

A One Ten Station Wagon in service at London's Heathrow Airport in the mid-Eighties.

A rarity was the One Ten with selectable four-wheel drive. This picture shows the unique transfer box lever fitted to such vehicles.

The distinctive grille badge of an early One Ten.

Early One Tens come together on the assembly track at Solihull during 1983.

CHAPTER 3

A Phoenix arises

Going into Europe, 1986-90

Tony Gilroy's reorientation of Land Rover towards Europe was probably the most fundamental change in the whole history of the marque. Always designed primarily as a utility for developing countries, the Land Rover was in fact totally different from the four-wheel drives which sold well in Europe. Solihull's approach had traditionally been a sober and strictly practical one; but the vehicles which had conquered continental European markets had side stripes, chrome and wide wheels to convey an image of their owners. This was not what Land Rovers had been about at all. Moreover, buyers on the European continent expected their vehicles to be capable of high speeds for long distances over European motorways – whereas Land Rover design had always concentrated on low-speed ability in rough terrain and had considered maximum speeds of under 70mph to be perfectly adequate for road use. Finally, tax laws and fuel costs in Europe had made the 4x4 market overwhelmingly diesel-oriented – the very area where Land Rover products were weakest.

Getting to grips with these new requirements was quite difficult for some of Land Rover's longer-serving people, because they demanded a radical change in approach. Yet Tony Gilroy insisted that, in the rush to conquer new markets, Land Rover should not abandon its traditional virtues. Those customers who wanted a rugged four-wheel drive utility must still be able to buy it from Solihull, and the most cost-effective way of achieving this was for Land Rover to build vehicles which both retained the strengths on which the marque had been built and appealed to the very different European market. It was a tall order, but it was to be the ethic which would shape the Land Rovers of the future.

New programmes
For the moment, there could be no question of radically new products; instead, Land Rover needed to put improved versions of its existing vehicles on the market with the minimum possible delay. So it was that, as early as 1984, the first programmes for gearing the Ninety and One Ten for better European sales were put into motion. On the one hand, Project Falcon was set up to provide the Land Rover utilities with a turbocharged diesel engine which would make them more competitive with the best-selling diesel-powered models then sold in Europe; and on the other, Project Capricorn embraced a whole series of primarily cosmetic improvements to the vehicles. Work also began on a 2.5-litre edition of the four-cylinder petrol engine, the very engine which had expressly been ruled out as a future possibility in the December 1983 Product Bulletin which had advised dealers of the forthcoming 2.5-litre diesel.

Nor was this all. Considerable effort was also devoted to the Range Rover to improve its European sales – notably with the introduction of a turbocharged diesel alternative to the V8 petrol engine – and to prepare it for its 1987 launch in the USA. In 1986, the final element of Land Rover's new-model strategy was put into place when the go-ahead was given for Project Jay, which materialized as the Discovery in 1989.

New ownership

Yet these were turbulent times for Land Rover. Tired of the financial drain on its resources which the nationalized British Leyland had represented since 1975, the British Government began in 1985 to consider ways of selling the company into private ownership. By the end of the year, the favoured plan was to divide BL into smaller packages and to sell them to the highest bidder. Land Rover had just begun to turn in a modest profit once again, and its future plans made it appear the most attractive of all the BL divisions for sale. Several British buyers came forward with bids, including Lonrho and Aveling Barford, and Land Rover's own management also put together a bid to buy the company.

However, by February 1986, the Government was favouring an offer from General Motors in America – primarily because GM was also willing to take the loss-making Leyland Vehicles truck and bus division. When the news became public, Land Rover devotees mounted a "Keep Land Rover British" campaign; MPs gave Trade and Industry Secretary Paul Channon a hard time in the House of Commons; and the British press indulged in one of its periodic bouts of patriotism. Frightened by the outcry, the Government backed down and the GM negotiators returned to the USA. It had been a close thing; but back at Solihull, the scare over the proposed sale actually strengthened morale within the company, and within Britain as a whole it strengthened public awareness of Land Rover's achievements. When British Leyland did eventually pass into new ownership in 1989, Land Rover was an integral part of the sale to British Aerospace of what was by then called the Rover Group.

1986: V8 Ninety and 2.5-litre petrol engine

Of course, continental Europe was never intended to be the only beneficiary of Land Rover's change of image. The home market was also under attack from Japanese four-wheel drives, which were vastly outselling the Ninety Station Wagons in the three-door short-wheelbase passenger-carrying 4x4 sector. So Land Rover resolved to

When the British Government threatened to sell Land Rover into American hands during 1986, enthusiasts responded with a massive campaign of opposition. This is one of the stickers from the campaign.

There was no mistaking the Diesel Turbo models from the rear – although the concentration on the 'Turbo' rather than the 'Diesel' was an interesting marketing trick! This type of decal was used on 1987 models only; the 1988 and later Diesel Turbos had the word 'turbo' in lower-case letters.

fight back and, with the V8-powered Ninety it announced in May 1985, the company delivered the first of a series of hugely effective counter-attacks.

The idea of a V8-powered short-wheelbase Land Rover was not new, although the V8 Ninety was the first example to reach production. As early as 1966, Solihull's engineers had dropped a Buick V8 into a Series IIA 88-inch model to see what the results would be, and the Rover Company's US subsidiary had performed a similar experimental conversion. There were experimental short-wheelbase models with V8 engines around right through the Seventies, and a handful of Stage 1 V8 88s were built around 1980 in anticipation of an overseas contract. So when Land Rover management gave the green light for the development of a production V8 Ninety, the model did not take long to develop. The product planners saw the V8-powered short-wheelbase model as an important image booster, and correctly anticipated that it would sell best to the recreational four-wheel-drive market, primarily in Station Wagon form. Nevertheless, the V8 engine was made

available in other Ninetys for the minority who wanted it.

The 3.5-litre V8 in the Ninety came in the same 114bhp, 185lb.ft tune as in the One Ten V8, but it was now equipped with electronic ignition to help maintain tune for longer periods and to give easier starting. It also came with a new gearbox: instead of the old Range Rover four-speed, the vehicle had a new five-speed overdrive box which vastly improved its cruising abilities. This was not the LT77 type already available in the four-cylinder models – which Solihull still doubted was strong enough to stand up to heavy-duty use behind the V8 engine – but rather the LT85 type built by Santana, Land Rover's licensees in Spain. Rather ironically, this gearbox had been designed at Solihull earlier in the decade to meet the Spanish company's need for a gearbox to suit European road conditions! Along with the electronic ignition, the new gearbox was also added to One Ten V8s when the V8 Ninety was announced.

The difference which the V8 engine and five-speed gearbox made to the Ninety was startling. What had been a plodder in the old Land Rover tradition with the 74bhp

33

2.3-litre petrol engine was suddenly transformed into a sprightly machine, capable of maintaining high motorway averages with ease. In fact, a Ninety V8 could reach 60mph from a standing start more quickly than a carburetted Range Rover! What was more, the low-down grunt of the V8 also satisfied those who wanted off-road ability. Contemporary reports were hugely enthusiastic about the vehicle, although most of them did spot that the gearchange was slow and notchy, which could make town driving rather tiring. In a comparison with the LT77 gearbox – itself no paragon of virtues – the LT85 certainly came a poor second.

While the Ninety V8 was a great image-booster for Land Rover in Britain, far more important in continental Europe was the more powerful four-cylinder petrol engine announced for both Ninety and One Ten models in October 1985. With the same 2.5-litre capacity as the recently enlarged diesel engine, it was small enough not to incur the tax penalties which ruled the 3.5-litre V8 out of contention in several European countries, and its additional

power brought welcome improvements in road performance.

Although Land Rover had foreseen no need for additional performance from the four-cylinder petrol engine at the end of 1983, when that Product Bulletin had confidently asserted that no 2.5-litre edition was planned, the subsequent drive for European sales had changed the picture. The fact that the petrol and diesel engines shared common design features made the development of the enlarged petrol engine that much simpler – and quicker. Its stroke was lengthened by the same amount as the diesel's had been to give the same 2,495cc capacity; a similar toothed-belt camshaft and auxiliary drive replaced the original roller chains; and once again lightweight alloy castings were used for the front cover and water pump casing.

Power went up by around 12% to 83bhp, while torque increased by nearly 11% to 133lb.ft, at 2,000rpm instead of the 1,800rpm of the older engine. Once again, the benefits were seen in improved acceleration and higher cruising

The Garrett turbocharger was mounted high up on the engine, as this underbonnet shot of an early Diesel Turbo shows.

This 1987-model Ninety County Station Wagon shows off that season's cosmetic improvements. Note the side decals (which would last for just one year) and the Range Rover-style spoked steel wheels. This example is a V8 (as the special decal at the rear shows), and the protruding snout covers the extra fans for an optional air conditioning installation.

speeds, and the new engine made the four-cylinder petrol Land Rovers that important bit more competitive with their petrol-engined Japanese rivals on the European continent. Gradually, the Land Rover marque was being strengthened – and the important new turbodiesel engine which would make it fully competitive in Europe was now just around the corner.

1987 models – facelift, uprated V8 and Diesel Turbo

None of the 1987 model-year changes to the Ninetys and One Tens, important as they were, had anything like the significance for Land Rover of the new turbocharged diesel engine. From October 1986, the results of Project Falcon went on sale in new models which wore Diesel Turbo badging to help differentiate them from the turbodiesel Range Rover, badged as a Turbo D.

There were good reasons for this distinction in badging because the Range Rover had a completely different engine bought in from VM Motori in Italy. In an ideal world, Solihull would have liked to use this much more powerful

engine in the Ninety and One Ten as well, but the costs were prohibitive. So it was that Project Falcon had been initiated to develop in-house a turbocharged edition of the long-serving Land Rover diesel engine.

The diesel engine had already been enlarged to 2.5 litres, and it was this engine which the Falcon team used as their starting-point. They doubtless looked at the turbocharged 2.25-litre engine which Santana had put on the market in Spain a few years earlier, and they certainly examined a turbocharged 2.25-litre engine built experimentally at Solihull in 1962. This one was actually in a preserved prototype owned by the museum collection now known as the Dunsfold Land Rover Trust!

However, there was much more to engineering the turbocharged engine than bolting a turbocharger onto the existing 2.5-litre diesel. The cylinder block had to be redesigned to incorporate an oil feed and drain for the turbocharger, and the crankshaft was cross-drilled to improve the lubrication of the bearing journals. There were new pistons and piston rings, and nimonic exhaust valves were specified to cope with the higher combustion temperatures associated with turbocharged engines. For the same reason, the water cooling system was uprated and fitted with a viscous-coupled fan, while an oil cooler became standard equipment.

The turbocharger chosen was a Garrett AiResearch T2 model, with integral wastegate limiting the boost to 10psi. The fuel pump was a self-priming DPS type with a boost control capsule and a cold-start timing retard device, and weight had been saved by a new alloy-bodied vacuum pump for the brake servo and by a lightweight starter motor which also gave higher cranking speeds. Lastly, there was a new air cleaner, which breathed through an intake on the left-hand front wing – a feature not found on other Land Rover models.

The primary design aim had been to increase the bottom-end torque to give good acceleration, and with these changes the engineers achieved a 25% increase in maximum torque together with excellent accelerator response and minimal turbo lag. Power also went up by 28% to give a noticeable improvement in high-speed cruising ability. With the five-speed gearbox, these characteristics created precisely the kind of vehicle the European market wanted, and the success of the Diesel Turbo was plain for all to see in sales figures. The abysmal results for the 1986 calendar-year were the end of the decline: 1987 saw production rise to meet the anticipated increase in sales, and from 1988 sales would continue to climb until the end of the decade. Land Rover had turned the corner.

Of course, the Diesel Turbo models alone were not responsible for this upward trend. The October 1986 changes for the 1987 model-year had also embraced a number of further specification improvements which made their own contribution to Land Rover's recovery. These included the first of many facelifts (in fact, part of the Capricorn programme) and the introduction of a more powerful version of the V8 petrol engine.

The 1987-season facelift gave all the Ninetys and One Tens new one-piece doors with more car-like handles, which replaced the recessed type, while painted body cappings and rain gutters took over from the earlier galvanized items. (This cosmetic change, it must be said, did nothing for the durability of the components affected.) County Station Wagons took on new side decals – the third type in four years – and Ninety County models were supplied as standard with an enamelled version of the steel Rostyle wheel originally designed for the Range Rover. Detail touches included a new fuel filler cap with optional keylock, a single-point twin-jet washer for the windscreen, and a relocated rear window washer nozzle on Station Wagons; Diesel Turbo models also carried a 'Turbo' decal at the rear. Meanwhile, a new radio housing was fitted to the centre of the dashboard on County models and others ordered with De Luxe cab trim.

The changes for 1987 were not all cosmetic, however: there were chassis improvements, too, as a tubular gearbox crossmember replaced the original rectangular type and a tubular steering guard was fitted. Under the bonnet, buyers of V8-engined Land Rovers found a significantly more powerful edition of the V8 engine, with a new camshaft and with twin SU carburettors replacing the twin Strombergs. This gave 134bhp – more than recent carburetted Range Rovers had boasted. Solihull was now giving those markets which took the One Ten in V8 form the sort of road performance they wanted.

This combination of new features – facelift, uprated V8, and Diesel Turbo – worked the miracle for which Land Rover had been hoping. Sales had been slipping every year since 1980, but during the 1987 model-year, Land Rover sales actually began the increase which would be fully reflected in the 1988 figures. With the new Range Rover Turbo D also on stream since April 1986 and Land Rover's dealer network in Europe being considerably strengthened, the company had left the doldrums of the early Eighties behind, and it had established a real presence on the continent.

Promoting the image
Land Rover was in no hurry to introduce its 1988 utility models. The Ninety and One Ten were selling strongly enough, and the only real piece of news at Motor Show time in October 1987 was a negative one: the old naturally-

Land Rover built the Cariba concept vehicle to show how the workhorse Ninety could serve as the platform for a leisure-oriented image 4x4. However, it would be many years before the ideas behind this one-off would see production.

aspirated 2.5-litre diesel disappeared from the home market options list. Nevertheless, it would remain available for overseas customers who mistrusted turbochargers, and would continue to be found on the Solihull production lines until December 1991, as Land Rover gradually completed assembly of a large fleet order for the British Army.

However, public interest in Land Rover's doings was held by the announcement of a strikingly attractive concept vehicle in the autumn of 1987. Keen to show that Solihull was now in touch with the tastes of the younger, image-conscious 4x4 buyer, PR chief Brian Townsend allowed the motoring press to try out the first of what he intended to be a small series of promotional vehicles.

This vehicle was known as the Land Rover Cariba, and was deliberately created as a Land Rover equivalent of weekend fun 4x4s like the Suzuki SJ. Using existing production parts and accessories as far as possible, it was designed to show what could be achieved by picking and mixing items already available from Land Rover. That also helped to keep build costs down, which was just as well

because Townsend's budget was strictly limited.

In fact, the vehicle which would become the Cariba was taken from the press demonstrator fleet in the first part of 1987, and was converted by the team which serviced and maintained the press vehicles and others owned by Land Rover. Starting life as a Ninety V8 soft-top with County trim, it was declared redundant as a demonstrator on the grounds that such models would be discontinued when the 1988 models went on sale! As converted, the Cariba featured a rollover bar braced to the windscreen header rail, wide tyres on aftermarket spoked wheels, a special interior using retrimmed Range Rover leather seats, and a unique metallic paint finish based on two contemporary Range Rover options. A military-specification swingaway spare-wheel carrier was mounted to the side-opening rear tailgate, and the vehicle was topped off by a custom-made soft-top and tonneau cover.

The Cariba was so enthusiastically received that Land Rover decided to look at the concept rather more seriously. So a second vehicle was built, this time by Land Rover's

The Cariba was billed by Land Rover as the 'Sunshine concept car'.

of image.

The new season's models brought mainly cosmetic differences, and the main focus was on the County Station Wagons which Land Rover hoped would strengthen its presence in the market sector where the still-secret Discovery would be launched in 1989. All the 1988 models had black bumpers in place of the galvanized-finish variety which had been standard wear since the very first Land Rovers had been built in 1948. On the workhorse models, these were complemented by a black grille, black headlamp surround panels and black wheelarch eyebrows. On County Station Wagons, however, the grille, headlamp surrounds and wheelarch eyebrows were all finished in the body colour.

The County models also picked up new side stripes yet again – the fourth variety since 1983 – and a Britax sunhatch over the front seats. This had a dot-screened glass panel which could be tilted into one of three positions or taken out completely. The sunhatch could also be ordered as an extra-cost option on other Land Rover models, and Land Rover Parts and Equipment offered an accessory pack to go with it. This consisted of a wind deflector, a storage bag for the glass panel and a clip-on interior sunblind which doubled as an insulation and trim panel.

Other, more minor exterior changes distinguished the 1988-model Land Rovers from their predecessors. Arrow Red and Shire Blue were added to the paint options list, although, as they replaced three colours from the 1987 range, the total number of paint options actually went down from eight to seven. Diesel Turbo models had a new decal on the rear panel, in lower-case letters, and a 'V8' decal was added to 3.5-litre models. Interior changes meanwhile contributed to an even more car-like ambience. Grey seat facings were complemented by dark grey door trim panels and carpets, while headlinings, when fitted, were in a lighter grey. The steering wheel boss was mildly altered, having horizontal styling lines above and below the Land Rover name instead of a recessed centre panel. Its rim was trimmed with leather on County Station Wagons, which also came with a stereo radio-cassette player as standard equipment. Last, but by no means least, there were

Special Vehicle Operations division, and was finished rather more soberly in white, with less expensive cloth upholstery. What prevented the concept from being taken further was simply cost: there was no way in which a Ninety V8 with the special features of these vehicles could be manufactured and sold at a price remotely competitive with the Suzuki and similar Japanese vehicles. So the two vehicles were sold off and the idea was put on ice – although it was revived in the early Nineties for the Defender, as Chapter 4 reveals.

1988: another facelift

The 1988-model Land Rovers made their appearance at the Royal Smithfield Show which opened on December 6, 1987, the choice of this prestigious agricultural show serving to reaffirm Land Rover's commitment to the agricultural market which had been its bedrock support in Britain for so long. The messages presented by the Cariba concept vehicle and the importance Land Rover attached to the Smithfield Show were unmistakable: what the company was saying was that it remained committed to building practical, durable and rugged vehicles, and was simply broadening their appeal by grafting on the additional quality

The black bumper, body-colour grille and headlamp surrounds, and yet another variety of side decal mark this One Ten County out as a 1988 model. The new sunhatch was also new for that season. Confusingly, this pre-release example was registered by Land Rover at the same time as the late example of a 1987-season Ninety County pictured on page 35.

Cloth upholstery was one of the 1988-season improvements...

... and the steering wheel was slightly modified. The central radio housing seen here was one of the previous season's improvements.

improved window seals for all models, which closed over the windows when these had been wound down into the doors and so sealed the door cavities more effectively.

1989: more stripes, fewer rivets

Introducing the new season's models in two stages allowed Land Rover to get two bites at the publicity cherry, and so only the 1989-model Range Rovers were introduced at Motor Show time in the autumn of 1988. The 1989-model Ninety and One Ten were once again announced at the Royal Smithfield Show, which this year opened on December 4. Although the changes were few in number, they represented an important step in the process of refinement which would turn the coil-sprung Land Rovers into Land Rover Defenders some 20 months later.

There were further revisions to the paint options for all models, and side-stripes now became standard across the Ninety and One Ten range: County Station Wagons retained those introduced in December 1987, but the utility models had new stripes which incorporated a large '90' or

'110' identifier. Rostyle wheels, already standard on Ninety County Station Wagons, now became an extra-cost option for all Ninetys. Optional on the cheaper vehicles but standard on both Ninety and One Ten County models was a new radio-cassette which incorporated a Long Wave receiver and a pre-set facility for 16 stations.

Probably the most noticeable change for the 1989-season Land Rovers affected only the hardtop and Station Wagon versions. The rivet-heads in the upper body sides of these models had always been a reminder of the Land Rover's essentially utilitarian nature, and had always seemed a little out of place on vehicles with the pretension to refinement of a County Station Wagon. So, for 1989, the upper body sides were redesigned to leave no rivet-heads exposed, a refinement which left the vehicles looking much less utilitarian.

In addition, Ninety hardtops could now be ordered with an optional Roof Appointment Pack – a rather grandiose name for what was no more than the complete roof and trimmings from the Ninety County Station Wagon. It

The Ninety hardtop showing off its rivet free upper body panels.

For 1990 and the last of the pre-Defender models, the plate badges above the grille lost the Land Rover name, which moved to an oval badge lower down. Neither the centrally-placed blue light nor the rope cleat were standard equipment, of course: the vehicle pictured is actually an airfield fire tender with a number of special features.

included Alpine lights, the tilt-and-remove sunhatch and the full Station Wagon style of headlining.

1990: badging changes

The big news from Land Rover in the autumn of 1989 was, of course, the launch of the Discovery, which was introduced at the Frankfurt Motor Show in September – that choice of venue reflecting Land Rover's continental European focus. As there were also important upgrades for the Range Rover at the same time (two new engines and ABS), there can have been little money left to spend on the utility Land Rovers. Their turn for specification changes would come the following year.

So for 1990, there were just two distinguishing changes for the Ninety and One Ten. The first was the arrival of repeater flasher lamps on the front wings as standard; such lamps had, of course, been a feature of the vehicles built for certain overseas markets for some time. The second change was to the badging, and it was a change which reflected the way in which Land Rover was raising its profile as a marque. During 1988, the company had started to use a new logo, with the marque name on a green oval, and the 1990 Land Rovers wore this oval on their grille slats, offset to one side. The silver-on-black plate above the grille changed at the same time, losing the Land Rover marque name and reading only '90' or '110'. From now on, numbers would take over from the established names of Ninety and One Ten, as part of the preparations for the Defender's introduction in the autumn of 1990.

Ring in the new
The steady climb in Land Rover sales in the later Eighties said everything that was necessary about the success of Tony Gilroy's business strategy. After sales had bottomed out in the middle of the decade, they began to reflect Land Rover's gains in Europe. The slide had been halted, and although sales of the coil-sprung models remained for the rest of the decade below their 1985 levels, they were on an upward trend. Only 1990 – a bad year for the motor

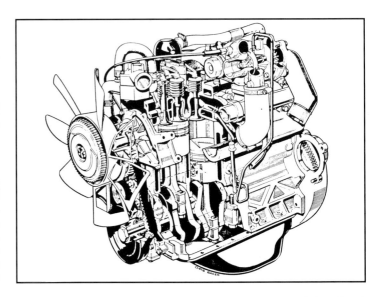

A revealing cutaway of the Diesel Turbo engine announced in 1986.

The air intake was carefully positioned behind the front wheelarch on Diesel Turbo models and served as a distinguishing feature. This example is a genuine ex-Camel Trophy vehicle and is equipped with a snorkel-type breather, a winch, a heavy-duty roof rack, a bullbar and additional lighting.

This 1988-model Ninety County Station Wagon carries a winch, neatly mounted just below the front bumper.

This Ninety soft-top was specially prepared as a commemorative vehicle for Land Rover's 40th Anniversary in 1988. Note the appropriate registration number.

industry in general, as the boom period of the late Eighties came to an end – showed a slight fall, and by then Land Rover had the astonishing success of the Discovery on its hands. In fact, 1990 broke all records for Land Rover's *total* vehicle production by a substantial margin.

It was sad, then, that the man who had brought about the company's salvation was no longer there to see the fruits of his success. Managing Director Tony Gilroy left the company during 1988, shortly before the whole Rover Group was purchased by British Aerospace. After that, there was further considerable upheaval as the Land Rover and car sides of the business were more closely integrated; from now on, Solihull would have a centralized management which was shared with Rover Cars. If Land Rover moved into the Nineties as a less independent entity within the Rover Group, it was nevertheless in a stronger position to draw on the expertise accumulated by Rover car engineers, marketing and sales people than it had ever been in the lifetime of the first-generation coil-sprung Land Rovers.

This One Ten Turbo Diesel Station Wagon was taken on by the Royal Berkshire Fire and Rescue Service in 1990, and carries body modifications by Locomotors of Andover. It is seen here towing a Breathing Apparatus support trailer.

A pair of utility models of the late Eighties, both on the 110-inch wheelbase. The model in the foreground has the High-Capacity Pick-up body and a window soft-top, the latter option of which was not available in the UK. In the background is a right-hand-drive 110 pick-up with standard tilt.

CHAPTER 4

Second generation

Defender 90 and 110

As part of the strengthening of the marque image which was initiated in the later Eighties, Solihull decided that its utility models should have a proper model-name of their own. The idea was that the name of Land Rover should become identified with the marque rather than too closely with just one of its products. After the introduction of the Discovery in 1989, it was clear that the term 'a Land Rover' no longer automatically meant one of the traditional utilities, because the Discovery also bore the Land Rover name.

A major package of changes to the coil-sprung utilities was at that time in the planning stages, and it would make sense to introduce the new model-name on these. So the search for a name began. According to representatives of Land Rover's US subsidiary, the name of Defender was thought up in a bar in downtown Boston when some of the Solihull management were visiting! It was a name which had definite merits, hinting at the peacekeeping role in which so many military Land Rovers were seen.

So the revised utility Land Rovers announced on September 11, 1990 and introduced to the public at the Birmingham Motor Show on September 22 became the first Land Rover Defenders. Also new at that show were the five-door body and fuel-injected V8 engine for the Discovery, and the limited-edition Range Rover CSK – quite a feast for Land Rover enthusiasts. Solihull might well have preferred to hold the new Defenders over until the Royal Smithfield Show in December, but that month would see the announcement of the 1991-model Range Rovers and Land Rover wanted the full glare of publicity on them

because they were likely to bring in more profit for the company than the Defenders would!

In any case, Solihull had some difficulty in making the Defenders look very different from the models they replaced. The important changes were under the skin, and so Land Rover dressed the vehicles up with a number of cosmetic alterations. Most visible were colour-keyed side decals, all prominently displaying the Defender name alongside '90', '110' or 'County' as appropriate. The grille badge was also new, and carried the Defender name without any indication of wheelbase length, while the old decal logo on the rear panel had been replaced by a plastic green oval badge. There were also two new body colours – a replacement white and a new grey.

The changes to the interior of the vehicles were nevertheless of very real benefit. The first one to catch the eyes of visitors to the 1990 Motor Show was the new cubby box between the driver's and passenger's seats, incorporating a trinket tray and a lockable glove box. As an alternative to the basic grey vinyl upholstery came brown Moorland dog-tooth cloth trim, and the front seats on all models were each positioned 25mm nearer the centre-line than before, to give the elbow-room between seat and door which the Ninetys and One Tens had always lacked. The cab doors also operated an interior courtesy light for the first time in a Land Rover utility, but the press-switches were rather flimsily mounted and soon gave trouble in service. Instruments and controls remained generally unchanged, although there was an improved wash/wipe

This early Defender 110 County Station Wagon shows off the grille badging which was always the easiest way of distinguishing Defenders from the earlier coil-sprung models. Side decals were also new, incorporating the Defender name, and just behind the front wheelarch is a small 'Tdi' decal to show that this model has the engine which would quickly become the most popular in the new models.

programme for the windscreen.

The most important new features of the Defenders lay in their drivetrains, however. Out went the old LT85 Santana gearbox, and in its place on V8 models came a newly strengthened edition of the LT77 five-speed which was also made standard on all other Defenders. The 2.5-litre petrol engine and the 2.5-litre naturally aspirated diesel were relegated to special-order only (and thus disappeared from the range to all intents and purposes), the 3.5-litre V8 remained unchanged with 134bhp, and the Diesel Turbo was replaced completely by a detuned version of the 200Tdi turbodiesel engine which had first been seen in the Discovery a year earlier.

The 200Tdi engine was a remarkable piece of machinery. Work had started on it in 1984, when Tony Gilroy had accepted the recommendation of his product planners that a new diesel engine would be necessary if Land Rover intended to compete seriously in Europe. Although the engine was first seen in the Discovery, it was intended from the beginning to suit the utility models as well – and in due

course it would also replace the Italian-built VM turbodiesel in the Range Rover. Right from the start, Land Rover took the bold decision to go for a direct-injection design because this would give much better fuel economy than the indirect-injection types which were then universal in diesel 4x4s; the downside was that direct-injection engines are always noisier and rougher than their indirect-injection counterparts, and indeed those always would be failings of the original engine.

The project to develop the new engine was known as Gemini. The designers started with the same bore and stroke dimensions as the then current Land Rover 2.5-litre diesel engine had, but ended up redesigning the block around them, among other things including an aluminium ladder-frame to improve its rigidity. The direct-injection cylinder head was designed in conjunction with specialists AVL in Austria, and the latest Bosch two-spring injectors and VE distribution pump were used. The engine was designed from the outset to be turbocharged, and the Garrett T25 turbocharger selected was complemented by an air-to-air intercooler which improved fuel combustion to the benefit of both acceleration and fuel economy.

In Discovery tune, the engine developed 111bhp and 195lb.ft of torque – the latter figure being rounded up to 200 to give the number in the 200Tdi name. The letters Tdi stood simply for Turbocharged, Direct-injection, and Intercooled. For the Defender, the turbocharger was repositioned higher up in order to fit comfortably in the engine bay, and the engine was detuned slightly to produce 107bhp and 188lb.ft of torque – mainly to make the paper specification of the Discovery look better if customers were trying to decide between that vehicle and a County Station Wagon. Even in this state of tune, the 200Tdi offered 26% more power and 25% more torque than the old Diesel Turbo engine of the same capacity – astonishing gains which appeared little short of miraculous when the 25% improvement in fuel economy and average 13% increase in maximum speed were taken into account!

Not surprisingly, the Defender Tdi quickly became the favourite model, although the V8 remained widely respected, particularly for Station Wagon models and particularly in those countries where its cubic capacity did not incur tax penalties. Body types remained as they had been for the Ninety and One Ten models in the 1990 model-year, with soft-top, hardtop, pick-up and Station Wagon types available on both wheelbases and an HCPU or long-wheelbase chassis. There was one deletion, however: the seven-seater County Station Wagon on the Defender 90 chassis was temporarily dropped from the range in order to protect sales of the new seven-seater Discovery.

Despite the excellence of these improvements, Defender sales did not improve on those of the models they replaced. Total sales for the 1990 calendar-year (which included both old-model Ninetys and One Tens and the new Defenders) were down over 1989, and sales would continue to decline gradually over the first half of the Nineties. The reason, mainly, was that there had been changes in the market-place. Many customers who might once have bought a Land Rover utility for agricultural or light industrial work

New decals were specified for the Defender 90s as well, with the stripes on the door sloping downwards instead of upwards as on the last of the old models. Just visible to the right of the spare wheel on this hardtop is the 'Defender 90' rear badging.

were now being tempted away by the cheaper Japanese 4x4s and in particular by the 4x4 versions of conventional pick-ups, such as Toyota's Hi-Lux. In addition, many customers who might once have bought a Land Rover County as a passenger-carrier were instead buying the very much more refined Discovery.

At Solihull, these changes must have been viewed philosophically. The Defender changes had undoubtedly prevented sales of the Land Rover utilities from slipping further, and in the meantime the Discovery and Range Rover were doing so well that profits were increasing all the time. Despite the fall in Defender sales, 1990 set records for *overall* sales of Land Rover products which would not again be broken until 1995.

1992-1993 models: minor changes
During the first three years of Defender production, the vehicle's specification changed in only small details. This was partly because there was not much more which could be done to the vehicle without expensive redevelopment

work, and partly because Solihull's designers and engineers were heavily committed on other projects. Not the least of these were improvements to the Range Rover and Discovery, the development of the completely new '38A' second-generation Range Rover, and work on a fourth model-range known as the CB40 project. As far as the Defender was concerned, there were two major projects under way: the first one to prepare the vehicle for its introduction to the USA, and the second one Land Rover's bid to win the contract for the next generation of light 4x4s for the British Army, which is discussed in more detail in Chapter 7. With all this consuming limited resources, it is hardly surprising that Solihull did not make more far-reaching changes to the basic Defender!

Nevertheless, there *were* changes. In January 1991, the front brakes of 90 and 110 variants were commonized, and the twin servo and master-cylinder assemblies were replaced by a common type. The next changes were announced in December that year, when Land Rover returned to the Royal Smithfield Show to introduce the 1992-model

For 1992, there were new side stripes yet again, as this long-wheelbase Station Wagon and short-wheelbase hardtop show.

The rigid spare-wheel centre cover seen here was introduced on 1993 model-year Station Wagons.

Defenders.

Changes at this stage were a new and smaller soft-feel two-spoke steering wheel, similar in appearance to the type fitted to the Discovery, and the standardization across the range of the power-assisted steering which had been optional on the 1991 models. Almost unnoticed (and even Land Rover press releases failed to mention it) was the improved LT77S gearbox, shared with manual Discovery and Range Rover models, which brought a better change action and less obstructive synchromesh. The starting-handle hole was deleted from the front bumper, and there were minor alterations to the sunhatch, which was still only optional on some models. Station Wagons acquired a map pocket on the rear of the driver's seat; yet another new style of side-stripes was introduced; and the four-cylinder petrol and the two older diesel engines were finally discontinued.

For 1993, there were only limited specification changes once again, the most notable being the deletion of the windscreen hinges (although a support bracket remained)

and the introduction of a stylized rigid spare-wheel centre cover on Station Wagons. Both, in fact, were part of the programme to adapt the Defender for sale in the demanding North American market, where Land Rover knew buyers would not welcome constant reminders of their vehicles' utility origins!

The NAS Defender 110
Back in the mid-Eighties, when Tony Gilroy had identified Europe and the USA as the two markets for Land Rover to target, it was quite clear which one should come first. For a start, Land Rover (and the related Austin-Rover Cars, as the division was then called) already had a small presence on the European continent; and secondly, Solihull's existing products needed relatively little redevelopment to make them properly competitive in Europe.

The USA, however, was a very different problem. Not only did Land Rover have no presence there, but its products would need major redevelopment before they

Prior to Defender introduction the 90 and 110 coil-sprung Station Wagons seen here were typical of the marque in the mid-eighties.

This 1989-model Ninety hardtop demonstrates the side stripes introduced on that season's utility models. The long-wheelbase types, of course, had a '110' identifier.

51

The first Land Rover utility to be sold in the USA since 1974 was this special-edition Defender 110, with 3.9-litre engine and external rollcage.

could be sold across the Atlantic. None of them met the tight US regulations on crash safety and exhaust emissions, and indeed Land Rover had pulled out of the USA in 1974 when it was unable to make the Series IIIs of the day meet those ever-tightening regulations. There was also the very important issue of quality: the poor panel-fits and other niggling problems with which Land Rover customers had learned to live over the years would have spelled instant rejection in the USA, where buyers had become accustomed to very high standards of build.

Land Rover determined to tackle the US market first with the Range Rover, and Project Eagle redeveloped that vehicle into one which achieved astonishing success in the world's toughest car market after its launch there in March 1987. So little known was the Land Rover name in the USA, that Solihull actually called its US subsidiary Range Rover of North America (RRNA) to avoid confusing buyers! However, all that was to change in the early Nineties, by which time the Range Rover was well-established in the US luxury market. From August 1, 1992,

RRNA changed its name to Land Rover of North America, and brought in the first of a specially-prepared limited edition of just 500 Defender 110s. Each one bore its limited-edition number on a special badge plate mounted to the rear panel.

In fact the NAS (North American Specification) Defender One Ten had been previewed at the Detroit Motor Show on January 8, 1992, even though sales did not begin until that autumn. The vehicle had been developed at Solihull by a small team under Colin Andrews, and it was very different indeed from the standard Defenders then on offer to the rest of the world. Its basis was the long-wheelbase V8 County Station Wagon, but instead of the 134bhp 3.5-litre carburettor engine the NAS Defender 110 Ten had the 180bhp 3.9-litre injected engine from the Range Rover. One reason for this was the increased performance which the engine gave, but equally important was the fact that this engine had already passed the US exhaust emissions tests and did not therefore need to be expensively redeveloped; the carburettor V8, by contrast, was not homologated for the USA.

Minor changes in lighting were also necessary for the Defenders to meet US traffic regulations, and to that end the front indicator lamps were relocated in the bumpers. These alone would have given the NAS (North American Specification) Defenders a distinctive appearance, but in fact another US requirement had resulted in a major feature totally unique on the Defender range. This was a tubular rollover cage positioned outside the body and supplied by Safety Devices. In its other markets, Land Rover was naturally not keen to explain that this had been fitted because the existing Defender body was not strong enough to pass the US rollover crash-safety test. Instead, it was presented as a cosmetic feature – and even in the USA it was described as an "expedition safari cage" to give the impression that it was a purely cosmetic addition!

Painted in dead white, with contrasting black wheelarch eyebrows and without the side decals standard on other Defenders, all the NAS 110s had air conditioning as standard. They could also be fitted with a wide range of

The injected 3.9-litre engine in the limited-edition North American Defender 110 was in contemporary Range Rover tune.

The interior specification of the North American Defender 110 included a radio/cassette unit in the centre cubby and extra instruments on the dashboard.

The High-Capacity Pick-Up remained available on the Defender 110 chassis throughout.

Among the South African-built curiosities was this One Ten Double Cab, built by the Safari Centre (see Chapter 6).

accessories, among them a Warn 8000 winch on the front bumper which was intended to add to their appeal as serious off-road adventure machines. Whether most of the Americans who paid what was really a very high price for them had any intention of venturing off the road is another matter; the fact was that these vehicles were sold as lifestyle accessories to the wealthy, who positively lapped them up. LRNA claims that 510 were sold (even though only 500 were originally promised), and the vehicle certainly performed a very useful service for Land Rover by establishing the marque name in the USA and associating it with ruggedness and real off-road ability. Encouraged by the success of the NAS 110, Solihull now started work on a second Defender for the USA.

The 90SV and the 1994 model-year
In the meantime, however, there was news on the home front. The experiments which had begun back in 1987 with the Land Rover Cariba concept vehicle had finally borne

fruit, and on June 4, 1993 Solihull announced the 90SV, the letters of its name taken from the Special Vehicles division which built it.

Like the Cariba, the 90SV was intended as a weekend fun vehicle, and like the Cariba it was based on the short-wheelbase chassis. Also, like the Cariba, it had a special paint job, in this case using a unique colour with the cumbersome name of Caprice Blue-Green Metallic. However, unlike the Cariba, it was diesel-powered, Solihull having recognized that the fuel economy of the 200Tdi engine was likely to have more appeal to the intended young buyers than the thirst of the 3.5-litre V8. All examples of the 90SV were built for the British market, and all therefore had right-hand drive.

The 90SV started life as a Defender 90 pick-up, and was then converted by Special Vehicles; the very nature of this operation meant that the model could only be produced in limited numbers. The basic vehicle was then equipped with a side-hinged tailgate and swingaway spare wheel, together

One of the first vehicles with the all-round disc brakes introduced for 1994 was the 90SV, a product of Land Rover's Special Vehicles division.

The one and a half millionth Land Rover utility was a Defender 90SV, which was driven off the assembly line by rock star Bryan Adams (standing in the vehicle, on the left). Strictly speaking, most of the one and a half million vehicles which preceded it were not Defenders but were Land Rovers plain and simple. PR staff at Solihull decided that message was too difficult to get across, however!

with a unique foam-covered external rollcage, similar in essentials to the one on the NAS 110. Accessories to fit its image were added, in the shape of a front bullbar (or 'nudge bar' in Land Rover's language) and full-length side steps ('side runners'). The interior was fitted out with County-style seats and a high-specification radio-cassette player with a removable face-plate. To finish the job, Special Vehicles provided a waterproof cotton-weave soft-top with roll-up side and rear windows.

This was, of course, just the base specification, and most examples of the 90SV probably had many of the extra-cost options. These included five-spoke 'Freestyle' alloy wheels of the type first seen on the Discovery, twin driving lamps, a tow pack, a front-mounted winch and a CD player: Land Rover had learned the value of offering a wide range of accessories from experience with the Discovery. Cost inevitably made the 90SV a relatively rare vehicle, as the buyers at whom it was aimed were mostly happy to spend considerably less money on a rather less able Suzuki 4x4 to promote a similar image of themselves. In fact, Land Rover

stopped advertising the SV after the end of the 1994 model-year, although it was theoretically still available to order from Special Vehicles. However, time would show that the 90SV was only the first of what Land Rover intended as a line of sports-utility vehicles for markets outside Great Britain.

Naturally, the 90SV was the centrepiece of the 1994-model Defender range, but it was not the only new vehicle to be introduced in June 1993. Now that the Discovery had moved into a rather higher price bracket, Solihull felt safe in reintroducing the seven-seat County Station Wagon on the short-wheelbase Defender chassis. This came as standard with Moorland cloth upholstery, a sunhatch, tinted glass and a radio-cassette player. Also new for the 1994 model-year was a 10-seater edition of the Defender 110 County, which provided four individual inward-facing rear seats, to give greater comfort than the two benches in the 12-seater model. The 12-seater nevertheless remained available for business users. Metallic and micatallic paints also figured in the options list for the first time.

The One Two Seven entered service with the RAF Regiment as a Rapier tractor (see Chapter 7), and is seen here with the weapons system in tow.

A Defender One Ten in the desert...potentially the perfect companion, although most travellers would make sure their vehicles are rather better-equipped than this one seems to be! The picture is, of course, a Land Rover publicity shot.

Despite the age of the basic design, the Defender 110 still looked clean and crisply styled by the time of this 1994-model Station Wagon.

A special rear nudge protection bar was cleverly integrated into the rear of the US Defender 110, disguised as a step! This picture also shows the special rear lights and, at top left, one of the points where the substantial rollcage goes through the body panels.

All the 1994-model Land Rovers also benefited from an important engineering change. Until this point, every coil-sprung Land Rover had featured disc brakes on the front wheels and drum brakes at the rear, but from June 1993, the rear brakes changed to discs and the front brakes on One Tens and on Ninetys with the High Load Suspension option became ventilated discs. The reasons were partly associated with the need for a bigger safety margin on forthcoming higher-performance models, and partly with the savings to be made by commonizing components with the Discovery and Range Rover. Undeniably, though, a specification which included all-disc brakes also had a powerful showroom appeal.

Meanwhile, a major milestone in Land Rover production was coming up fast. Land Rover had built its one millionth vehicle in 1976, and since then had built very nearly another half million. Exactly how those figures were worked out never has been clear, but they almost certainly included

US regulations called for a high-mounted stoplight on the Defender 110, an item not fitted to vehicles for other markets.

CKD vehicles assembled overseas and excluded vehicles made wholly overseas, such as the licence-built Santana Land Rovers. One way or another, it suited Land Rover very well to make a publicity splash at this stage, and the company held a small celebration at the end of the Defender assembly line on July 29, 1993.

The vehicle designated as the 1.5 millionth Land Rover was, unsurprisingly, a 90SV – which was, of course, not a line-built vehicle at all but a Special Vehicles confection! That vehicle was put back on to the assembly line and was driven off it by Canadian rock star Bryan Adams, whose enthusiasm for Land Rovers was widely known. The 1.5 millionth Land Rover itself (chassis number SALLDVAF7KA925966) was expected to join the Heritage Collection at its Gaydon museum after being used for publicity purposes.

The NAS 90

It soon became apparent that the basic design of the 90SV would be used in other spheres, and on September 3, 1993 a version of it was announced by Land Rover of North America as the follow-up vehicle to the previous year's hugely successful Defender 110 limited edition. For the USA, the vehicle was simply known as a Land Rover Defender 90 and, of course, qualified as a 1994 model; LRNA intended to sell it at the fashionable end of the

The NAS 90 had a number of special interior features many of which are shown in this cab shot.

This Ninety wears aftermarket wheels and tyres with an off-road bias to improve its rough-terrain ability.

The Cariba and the 90 SV inspired a number of home-made lookalikes, of which this Ninety is an example.

sport-utility vehicle (SUV) market which was then dominated by vehicles such as the Jeep Wrangler.

Like the NAS 110 and for the same reasons, the NAS 90 had the 3.9-litre V8 engine, by now slightly more powerful with 182bhp. The gearbox was, of course, the five-speed LT77S. There were ventilated disc brakes at the front, and the standard Freestyle sparkle-silver finish five-spoke alloy wheels wore chunky-looking BF Goodrich 265/75 R 16 Mud Terrain radial tyres. To improve the handling – and so that the vehicle would more precisely meet the expectations of the US 4x4 market – both front and rear axles were fitted with anti-roll bars. Similar installations had already been used on the Range Rover and Discovery, but this was their first-ever appearance on a regular-production Land Rover utility.

The general body configuration of the NAS 90 was similar to that of the 90SV, but the NAS front bumper with its integral indicator lamps was added, and the rear lamps were in rectangular clusters, quite unlike those of Defenders built for other markets. Quartz-halogen headlamps were also

fitted, and the rear panel had a unique 'Defender 90' badge while there were 'V8' decals behind the front wheelarches. Inside, the NAS 90 had reclining front bucket seats with head restraints, upholstered in a special weather-resistant Ash Grey twill material; between the front seats was a lockable centre cubby which also contained a top-quality radio-cassette unit. This came as standard with four speakers. Last but not least, there were rubber floor mats front and rear and a full tonneau cover.

As with the 90SV, Solihull hoped that customers would personalize their vehicles with a selection of accessories, and to that end a wide range was available. There was the so-called 'Bimini' half-top, essentially a canvas roof and rear panel for the cab area, and this could be complemented by a full cloth convertible top developed by Tickford, which consisted of door tops with sliding windows and a cloth soft-top over the rear rollcage. A forward-facing rear bench seat for two brought integral three-point safety belts, and a further option was an auxiliary heater for rear seat passengers. Full carpeting could also be ordered as an

The USA was also treated to a special soft-top version of the Defender 90, powered by the 3.9-litre V8 engine. This was the culmination of the idea which had begun many years earlier with the Cariba concept vehicle.

64

option and, of course, air conditioning was also available. The NAS 90 came in a range of bright colours associated with the Discovery and Range Rover models, together with its own unique AA Yellow.

The NAS 90 caused far more of a stir in the USA than the 90SV had done in Britain. Almost immediately after its launch, it was voted 'Four-Wheeler of the Year' by *Four-Wheeler* magazine, beating opponents from Isuzu (the Rodeo LS), Chevrolet (the K-2500 Suburban) and Ford (the Explorer Limited) by a huge margin. Although LRNA had cautiously introduced it as a limited-availability model, the company found itself importing the Defender 90 again for the 1995 model-year which began in December 1994, this time with a more powerful AM/FM radio-cassette unit (augmented later in the season by an optional CD autochanger), better sound insulation, map pockets in the doors and on the seatbacks, and the addition of Beluga Black clearcoat paint to the colour options. The 1995 models came with a removable fastback-style soft-top as standard and with an array of other soft-top options, all of them made by Bestop in the USA. These included a redesigned full soft-top, the Bimini half-top, and a surrey top for the cab area. In addition, there was the option of a unique removable GRP hardtop designed and manufactured in the USA in response to customer demand. Finished in Ash Grey to match the upholstery, this could also be bought as an accessory and fitted to earlier NAS 90s.

1995: the 300Tdi and the R380

Land Rover introduced its 1995 model-year changes well in advance of the traditional model-year start, announcing them on March 4, 1994. Changes made to the manual gearbox and the turbodiesel engine for the 1995-model Defenders reflected those made for the 1995-model Discovery and Range Rover at the same time. The LT77S five-speed gearbox was replaced by a new five-speed called the R380, its name standing for Rover (now that Land Rover and Rover engineering operations were closely integrated) and its maximum torque capacity of 380Nm (approximately 280lb.ft). Apart from the increased torque

capacity, the major advantages of this new gearbox were its light and precise shift action, accompanied by synchromesh on reverse gear. Reverse itself was now behind fifth instead of out to the left of first, giving a neater double-H gate pattern instead of the single-H with double dog's leg of the LT77S.

The turbodiesel engine was actually much more different

Defender chassis stacked at Solihull, awaiting their turn on the assembly lines. This picture was taken in August 1995.

The decal tells the whole story: this Defender is fitted with Land Rover's direct-injection turbocharged diesel engine.

from the earlier 200Tdi than its new name of 300Tdi might have suggested. Known internally as the Gemini 3 engine (Gemini 2 was another development which Solihull was not then prepared to discuss), it had the same bore and stroke dimensions and offered the same power and torque outputs as the 200Tdi it replaced; but it was actually a thoroughly redeveloped engine. In Defender form, it came this time in the same 111bhp, 195lb.ft tune as the Discovery and Range Rover versions; and the name of 300Tdi had been chosen purely as a marketing device rather than to reflect some massive increase in maximum torque!

The 300Tdi engine had no fewer than 208 new components as compared with the 200Tdi. These included the cylinder head, injectors, pistons, conrods, turbocharger, exhaust manifold, timing belt, water pump and alternator. Design aims, amply fulfilled in practice, had been to lower the noise levels for which the 200Tdi had been criticized, to meet all known and anticipated legislation about diesel

exhaust emissions worldwide, and to reduce build time and thus reduce manufacturing costs. The new engine also required less frequent servicing than the old, which, of course, brought savings to the customer as well.

The 1995-model Defenders also incorporated some more minor improvements. One which was long overdue was seat-belts on the inward-facing seats in the rear of Station Wagons; a modification to the clutch mechanism on all models lowered the effort needed at the pedal; there was improved interior lighting, and a better-specification radio-cassette unit was standardized.

Over in the USA, customers were also treated to yet another limited-edition model for the 1995 model-year which started in summer 1994. This was a Ninety Station Wagon, equipped like the earlier NAS 90 with a 3.9-litre V8 engine and kitted out with Freestyle alloy wheels and yet another set of special rear lamp units. From one point of view, limiting these vehicles to a run of 500 may have been a cautious exercise to test the market, but from another it looked like an astute marketing trick to build the image of exclusivity on which LRNA had been working for so long. Sales were encouraging enough to make Solihull prepare a further US-only Defender 90 for 1997 – although for 1996 the model was not available in the USA. That 1997 model, announced at the New York Motor Show in April 1996 but not scheduled to reach the showrooms until much later in the year, was to be a 90 Station Wagon with the latest 4-litre V8 (as seen in Range Rovers and Discoverys), an automatic transmission, and air conditioning as standard. A soft-top version was expected to follow in spring 1997.

A special engine for Europe
All this time, Land Rover had been plugging away to increase Defender sales, with – it must be said – considerable success. Worldwide sales of Defenders climbed by 8.9% from 19,375 in 1993 to 21,091 in 1994 (when Land Rover broke its 1990 overall vehicle sales record by a massive 38%). The results in Europe were most satisfying, and those in Italy particularly so. It therefore came as no great surprise when the company proudly announced in December 1994 that it had won a contract

This 1996-model Defender 90 County Station Wagon has the 300Tdi engine and the Freestyle alloy wheels which had become optional by that time.

against European competition to supply the Carabinieri with a fleet of 840 Defender 90s, beginning the following March.

What was unusual about these vehicles, however, was that they were to have engines not available as a showroom option: the 134bhp T16 2-litre petrol engine offered in various Rover cars and in the Discovery Mpi. The T16 was perhaps not the ideal engine for a vehicle of the Defender's type, being a high-revving four-valves-per-cylinder power unit without much of the bottom-end torque so expected in a Land Rover. However, the contract did reveal one important aspect of Solihull's policy in the mid-Nineties; namely, that the company was prepared to bend over backwards to sell Defenders in quantity to high-profile customers in important markets.

The 1996 models
For a time in the early Nineties, when Defender sales were

slipping, it had looked to many commentators as if the time was not far off when Land Rover would abandon its utility models altogether and concentrate on its more profitable Discovery and Range Rover models. The news that a fourth model range – the CB40 – was on the way also made motor industry analysts wonder how the company could possibly build so many different models on its already cramped Solihull site. After the Rover Group, and Land Rover with it, was sold by British Aerospace to the BMW company early in 1994, many people outside the company confidently expected the ruthlessly rational Germans to axe the Defender range.

Yet their expectations were not to be fulfilled so quickly, and over the summer of 1995 Solihull announced both a series of revisions to the regular production Defenders and then the new Defender XD range. The XD, developed for military use and described more fully in Chapter 7, would, of course, be sold on the civilian market as well if demand justified it, said a Land Rover spokesman at the time. Clearly, there was life in the old warhorse yet.

The 1996 models announced on June 12, 1995 finally introduced to the rest of the world the anti-roll bars first fitted to the NAS 90 two years earlier. These came as part of an option package, which was completed by the sparkle-finish Freestyle spoked alloy wheels and chunky BF Goodrich tyres also seen on the NAS 90. Other 1996-model changes mostly affected the County Station Wagons, which could be had with three new colours (Rioja micatallic red, Willow metallic olive green and Biarritz micatallic blue) and came as standard with an upgraded radio-cassette with removable face-plate which could also be fitted at extra cost to other Defenders. Meanwhile, a special limited-edition model was announced for the French market at the Val d'Isère international 4x4 show over the summer of 1995. Called the Land Rover Eastnor (Eastnor in Herefordshire is where Land Rover's well-known off-road test site is located), this was essentially a version of the NAS 90 equipped with the 300Tdi turbodiesel engine instead of the 3.9-litre petrol V8. Only 150 were planned, but no doubt Land Rover had every intention of building a few more if demand proved strong enough!

Epilogue

Even though they have sold in smaller numbers than previous Land Rover utilities, the Defender models of the Nineties have unquestionably been the best of their kind to come out of Solihull. Much easier to live with on an everyday basis than earlier Land Rovers, they have also offered greater road performance (from the NAS 3.9-litre V8) and greater fuel economy (from the 200Tdi and 300Tdi engines) than any of their ancestors. Sales in 1994 and 1995 also showed a revival which was simply astonishing for vehicles which were in essence well over a decade old. Whether their remaining production life is lengthy or truncated, the Defenders will always hold a special place in Land Rover history as the models which took the company into the fashionable end of the sport-utility market – and survived with their ruggedness and formidable off-road abilities intact.

Defender assembly at Solihull in the early Nineties. The building where these vehicles are built once housed assembly lines for the stately Rover P4 saloons, whose production ceased in 1964.

CHAPTER 5

Special vehicles

Including the One Two Seven and Defender 130

A lot was changing at Solihull as the coil-sprung models came on-stream. Even though the fundamental change to Land Rover Ltd had occurred as long ago as 1978, the early Eighties continued to see changes in the internal organization of the company. Among those was a change to the Special Projects department, and this had a far-reaching effect on the activities of the conversion specialists who had worked with Solihull's products for many years.

Special Projects had been set up in 1957 under George Mackie to oversee the work of the aftermarket converters who worked on Land Rovers. Its functions were to assist where possible with Land Rover-based conversions, to grant Land Rover Approval to those which would not compromise the integrity of the base vehicle (Approval meant that the standard Land Rover warranty would be honoured), and generally to act as a conduit between the customer with a special requirement and the converter who could supply it.

The system worked well for many years, but in 1981 George Mackie retired and was not directly replaced. Special Projects existed for a brief period as an element in the Engineering Department, continuing its traditional functions while the Series III Land Rovers remained in production. However, plans were laid at quite an early stage for those functions to change, and in 1982-83 Special Projects began to evaluate the One Ten as a platform for special conversions.

Many of the existing aftermarket conversions could be readily adapted to the new One Ten, and in their confidential descriptive brochure of September 1982, Special Projects were at pains to point out dimensions which had not changed on the new vehicles as well as those which had. However, by this stage the department had also started work on a special derivative of the One Ten which would be built in-house.

The Crew Cab

By the turn of the Eighties, Land Rover had become a company driven by its product planners – a very different company from the engineering-led Land Rover of earlier times. The function of the product planners was to identify gaps in the 4x4 market and to suggest ways in which the company might fill them. A brief would then be handed down to the engineers to develop the product to fill that gap.

However, things were not always as simple as that explanation makes them sound. Thus, when the product planners identified a market for a rugged 4x4 with a four-door crew cab capable of carrying five men and a high-capacity pick-up body for their equipment, they suggested to the Special Projects engineers that this might be fitted onto a Stage 2 Land Rover chassis with its wheelbase extended to 135 inches. The engineers' response was to point out that a wheelbase this long would demand expensive chassis reinforcement which would make the whole exercise uneconomical. Nevertheless, the concept was pursued, and in the end a viable vehicle was designed.

The crew cab was fairly simple to construct, using a

The stretched chassis was originally designed for the Crew Cab vehicle, with a five-man cab and pick-up body. This early example is equipped with the GRP Truckman Top, an approved accessory supplied by B Walker and Sons Ltd.

combination of truck cab and Station Wagon body parts. However, other dimensions had to be juggled quite carefully so that the stretched chassis would not be overloaded, and in the end the engineers settled on a wheelbase of 127 inches and a slightly shortened version of the High-Capacity Pick-Up rear body. Initial chassis development work was carried out in conjunction with Spencer Abbott, the Birmingham company which already produced long-wheelbase chassis conversions for the Range Rover. However, Land Rover wanted to build the 127-inch chassis in higher volumes than Spencer Abbott could cope with, and so all the production chassis were built in-house at Solihull.

Land Rover announced the 127-inch wheelbase model at the same time as the One Tens in March 1983, although it did not actually become available until the end of the year. It was called the One Ten Crew Cab, but never wore One Ten badging, instead having above its grille the simple 'Land Rover' nameplate which had been seen on the Stage 1 109-inch models.

During 1984 and the first half of 1985, the One Ten Crew Cab was built in fairly small numbers by the Special Projects department, each vehicle starting life as a One Ten chassis/cab and being converted and built up by hand. However, it rapidly became obvious that the 127-inch chassis had far greater potential as a basis for Land Rover conversions, and during this period Special Projects evaluated a small number of proposals put forward by the aftermarket converters. In the meantime, Tony Gilroy had replaced Mike Hodgkinson as Managing Director of Land Rover, and he had embarked on the ruthless drive for streamlining and efficiency within the company which would save it from terminal decline over the next few years. Not surprisingly, the work of Special Projects came under his scrutiny.

The birth of SVO

Gilroy's brief when he took over Land Rover was to maintain and improve the company's profitability in the face of declining sales worldwide, and he decided that more

70

of the profit in the conversions market could and should be coming Land Rover's way. So he set about reorganizing the Special Projects department and strengthening its role. From July 1985, the department was established as a separate business unit within Land Rover under its own chief engineer and with the new name of Special Vehicle Operations, or SVO for short. Its new head was Roland Maturi, formerly Land Rover's Director of Product Planning.

One major change had already been made since the creation of Land Rover Ltd in 1978. This was that a greater proportion of the approval test procedure costs had been passed on to the converters. The old Special Projects department had achieved this by introducing a process of 'self-certification', under which initial tests had to be carried out and funded by the converters themselves. Under SVO, however, two further changes would take place which would radically alter the face of the Land Rover conversions' business.

The first of these was that Land Rover would take a new position as the dominant partner in the relationship with its approved converters. Under the old system, the converters had been viewed more or less as equal partners with Land Rover in the production of a converted vehicle. Under SVO, it would be clear that the converters were simply supplying additions to the core Land Rover product. The second change was that Land Rover would bring a greater proportion of the conversion work back in-house. This meant that all work on the basic vehicle – primarily chassis modifications and some kinds of special bodywork – would now be done at Solihull. Only those converters which offered something Land Rover could not (such as specialist equipment) would be retained on the approved list.

The total package left Land Rover with much more control over the aftermarket than it had ever enjoyed before, and it caused an uproar in the conversions industry. As Solihull began to tighten its grip during 1984-85, several converters found their agreements with Land Rover were not renewed, or would be renewed only on different terms. The larger companies survived, but some of the smaller

Under SVO, the 127-inch chassis became the basis of a whole range of different conversions. This one has a crew cab and SVO's own Quadtec 1 low-roof box body.

ones disappeared from the Land Rover scene. Their places were taken by others who were prepared to play the game Land Rover's way.

Crew Cab becomes One Two Seven

Experience had shown Special Projects that not every Land Rover conversion was a one-off, despite the enormous variety of detail differences. Many conversions embodied common features, and in the early Eighties Solihull's product planners proposed that the division should develop core products which incorporated these.

So it was that while the converters were looking with great interest at the Crew Cab's chassis with its 127-inch wheelbase during 1984-85, work was also going on at Solihull to make the most of this new product. There had always been a demand for longer and larger Land Rovers, and during the Seventies, this demand had been satisfied by stretched Series III 109s with third-axle conversions. When all six wheels were driven, these vehicles offered formidable extra traction in rough terrain, but few customers actually

needed all that ability and the six-wheelers did have the disadvantages of being both rather cumbersome and forbiddingly expensive. The 127-inch chassis looked like a much more cost-effective and acceptable way of meeting demand for a larger Land Rover, and when SVO opened for business in 1985, the long-wheelbase chassis was one of its core products. The old One Ten Crew Cab name disappeared (although the model itself could still be had) and from this time on, all vehicles built on the stretched chassis were known as Land Rover One Two Sevens and wore 'Land Rover 127' badges.

SVO's second core product was a box body. Many special conversions demanded special bodywork as well as special chassis, and an analysis of the market suggested that the very simplest of box bodies would cater for most of them. So it was that four variations on a simple box were developed: SVO customers could order high-roof or low-roof types, and the boxes could be long (to suit a single-cab One Two Seven chassis) or short (to suit the crew-cab type).

SVO also approved 6x6 conversions such as this one.

The One Two Seven chassis was used as the basis of this Carmichael Fire Tender conversion. It has a V8 engine and belongs to the Royal Berkshire Fire and Rescue Service.

The box body quickly found an enthusiastic market. The first one was delivered to the Ministry of Defence, the second went to the BBC, and after that the orders flowed in. One well-publicized early vehicle was kitted out as a mobile workshop for Band Aid, and was shipped out to North Africa to help keep the charity's convoys of food trucks moving. Others found homes with high-profile users such as Police Forces in Britain.

Other conversions
The One Two Seven was, of course, not the only chassis available through SVO. Special conversions could also be built on One Ten chassis and even on the Ninety, although the latter was too small to be a popular basis for conversions. Some of these conversions were carried out at Solihull by SVO, although many were not. During its first

year in business, SVO signed several collabortion agreements with existing and new converters who would be able to supply equipment or vehicle bodies which Land Rover itself could not.

These conversions – no longer known as Approved Conversions – were all promoted with their own sales literature, and particularly striking about this was the low profile given to almost all the converters. The exception was Short Brothers of Belfast, whose Shorland armoured vehicles continued to be promoted as its own products. The other converters, however, figured only in the small print of the sales brochures, and in some cases as no more than a logo. So, for example, what had once been a Pilcher-Greene ambulance conversion on a Land Rover chassis was now called a Land Rover Ambulance. In no case did the sales brochures show the converter's address; interested customers were given only Land Rover as a point of contact. Solihull was now exerting a very firm grip on the conversions market.

Land Rover conversions in the Eighties

SVO offered a wide range of conversions during the Eighties, primarily on the One Ten and One Two Seven chassis. From the end of 1985 there was also a three-axle 6x6 model, derived from the Series III 6x6 conversion developed by Scottorn and sold under the Reynolds Boughton name after that company took over the Scottorn interests. This was listed for customers who needed the extra traction of the third driven axle and was never very common; as Solihull's product planners had expected, most customers for an extra-long Land Rover were quite content with the abilities of the 127 model.

The following list, which is not exhaustive, covers the most common conversions available through SVO during the Eighties. Details and pictures of many unusual or one-off conversions can be found in Richard de Roos' book, *Land Rover Conversions & Applications since 1948*, also published by MRP.

Ambulances	were available in three different varieties, all on the One Ten chassis. MMB International supplied a distinctive high-roof type based on a chassis/cab, while Pilcher-Greene's Type 8303 was built on a chassis/cab, but the firm's Type 8404 was a cheaper type based on a One Ten pick-up.
Backhoes	on the One Ten chassis/cab were supplied by Beaver.
Cash Guard Vehicles	were built by Glover Webb and had armoured van-type bodies on the One Ten chassis.
Discreetly Armoured Vehicles	were converted by MacNeillie from One Ten Station Wagons. The vehicles normally had four adjustable Range Rover front seats in place of the standard forward-facing seats.

Military Vehicles	were also constructed or commissioned through SVO (see Chapter 7).
Mobile Communications Units	were equipped by Agri-Visual and were based on One Ten hardtops or on One Ten Station Wagons. The three main models were a mobile cinema unit, a mobile video unit and a mobile public address unit, but other types were available to special order.
Mobile Work Platforms	were offered on the 6x6 chassis and were fitted with hydraulic lifts and cages by Spencer.
Multi-loaders	were the work of Skip-Tip Engineering Ltd. They were based on the One Two Seven chassis and had a pair of hydraulically operated arms at the rear. These could be used to lift a skip or pallet into position in the body which, when empty, could be used as a dropside lorry. If the skip was fixed rigidly to the hydraulic arms, the vehicle could be used as a tipper truck. Finally, it was possible to fit a hydraulic mixer (such as a cement mixer) between the arms at the rear.
Semi-tractors	with a fifth wheel for an articulated trailer coupling were based on the Ninety chassis/cab and supplied by H and J Potter of Chichester, using fifth-wheel couplings by Davies Magnet Works of Ware. They were mainly supplied to tow the starting-gates used in horse racing.
Towlifts	were fitted to the One Ten chassis/cab by Brimec Recovery Systems. At the rear they had a frame which could be lowered into place and reversed under the wheels of a vehicle. The frame and wheels were then raised to allow the vehicle to be towed. When not in use, the recovery frame was carried vertically at the rear of the vehicle.

This ambulance was built on a One Ten chassis in the mid-Eighties for an overseas customer by MMB International Ltd.

The Fourth Marque

Over the second half of the Eighties, SVO's place in the Land Rover business was gradually strengthened. The box-body concept was expanded, and the product was given its own brand-name of Quadtec. By the early Nineties, SVO had become what Roland Maturi liked to call the 'Fourth Marque' – a brand in its own right alongside the Land Rover utilities, the Range Rover and the Discovery.

SVO's work was, of course, not confined solely to the Land Rover utilities, because the division also had responsibility for conversion work on the two estate models. In addition, it undertook the assembly of some prototype vehicles (principally those which were modifications of existing production types, such as the Cariba-derived sport-utility Ninety described in Chapter 3), and it also prepared the Camel Trophy vehicles (see Chapter 8). Essentially, the

other divisions of Land Rover often turned to SVO when they needed a specially-equipped vehicle – and that was how SVO came to build a floating Land Rover in 1989.

The floating Land Rover never was intended to be a production option, although the principles behind its design were later used successfully to create a second floating vehicle – this time a Discovery – for publicity purposes. The floating Land Rover was created for Cowes week, the prestigious nine-day long summer regatta held at Cowes on the Isle of Wight and an event which always receives worldwide media coverage. As Land Rover had announced that it would be sponsoring the event for the next four years, the company intended to make maximum use of the publicity opportunities.

Land Rover had in fact built floating Land Rovers before, back in the early Sixties when the British Army was interested the idea. One of the prototypes still survived in the Dunsfold museum collection, and so SVO borrowed it back and examined how it had been built. They discovered that Avon could recreate the detachable inflatable airbags without too much difficulty, that not too much effort was needed to waterproof a modern Land Rover, and that with the aid of a propeller on the PTO output and a rudder at the rear the vehicle could even be 'driven' on the water. The result was that a 1988 Ninety Diesel Turbo soft-top was turned into a mobile advertising hoarding and floated up and down the harbour at Cowes between the yachts, parading the Land Rover logo in a most effective way on worldwide TV!

SVO and the Defender
Roland Maturi left Land Rover in 1991 and Chris Langton took over as the Director of SVO. Then in 1992, SVO was renamed as Land Rover Special Vehicles. Nevertheless, its functions throughout the early Nineties remained as they had been during the later Eighties: to handle all the non-line-build options and conversions for Land Rover products. Among these, in due course, would be the NAS One Ten models (see Chapter 2) and the 90SV (see Chapter 3), both of them limited-edition vehicles converted by hand from otherwise standard line-built models.

In the meantime, the Defender range had replaced the original Ninety and One Ten models, and SVO's One Two Seven had been renamed as a Defender 130. Engine availability was limited to the Tdi turbodiesel and the 3.5-litre carburettor V8, but otherwise the vehicle's specification was essentially unchanged from the One Two Seven of old. All that had happened was that the marketing people had decided it needed a more snappy name, and Defender 130 seemed to fit in better with Defender 90 and Defender 110 than Defender 127 would have done!

Nevertheless, the Defender 130 did differ from the Land Rover One Two Seven in one very important respect. From about the time when the Defender was introduced (the timing was probably not exact), the stretched utility Land Rover ceased to be an SVO conversion and became instead a line-built vehicle. As demand had crept up, so it had

More evidence of SVO expertise: this is the floating Land Rover Ninety, pictured by Dave Shephard in action at Cowes Week over the summer of 1989.

A Tdi-powered tipper on the Defender 130 chassis, dating from 1990.

"The world's longest Land Rover", according to the company's own publicity, was this 6x6 built by SVO for Eastern Electricity in 1991. It was 21 feet long and weighed-in at 2.8 tonnes unladen.

Visitors to the Heritage Motor Museum at Gaydon can catch one of two 'road trains' which have Defender 110 motive power. Special Vehicles co-ordinated the construction of their unique bodywork.

SVO were not involved in every Land Rover conversion, of course. This is one which was done independently. It is one of two Coyote models built by London coachbuilder Vantagefield in the late Eighties, incorporating several Range Rover body elements and a plush leather interior which features four individual Range Rover seats.

become increasingly difficult to accommodate the chassis conversion work alongside all the other work going on in the Special Vehicles division, and so the switch was made. True, the Defender 130 always left the lines as a chassis with bare bulkhead or as a chassis with either standard three-man or five-man crew cab, but it had nevertheless attained the status of a fully-fledged Land Rover vehicle rather than a conversion.

Land Rover Special Vehicles conversions

Several of the conversions on the Ninety, One Ten and One Two Seven chassis were, of course, carried over by SVO for the Defender models. Yet the range of conversions available continued to evolve. Those listed here were available from Special Vehicles in 1993. Like the SVO list on page 74, it does not claim to be exhaustive.

Ambulances	On the Defender 110, there were a two-berth model based on the pick-up, a coachbuilt Emergency Ambulance and a four-berth Field Ambulance for military use; all of these came with either Tdi or V8 engines. There was a low-cost Station Wagon-based ambulance conversion, which could also be supplied with a high roof; this came with Tdi, V8 or 2.5-litre petrol engines. MMB International supplied the coachbuilt body for the Defender 130 ambulance, which could also be had in high-payload military form with a strengthened rear chassis and axle, and with uprated road springs and brakes. An alternative military ambulance was based on Special Vehicles' own Quadtec 4 high-roof box body; for details of British Defender 130 military ambulances, see Chapter 7.
Cash Guard Vehicles	The Glover Webb bullion van based on a 110 chassis remained available.
Dropside Lorries	were available on the 130 chassis and could be fitted optionally with various cranes for loading.
Fire Engines	were converted by Pilcher-Greene, who offered the Branbridge MkIV (coachbuilt with three-

	man cab), MkV (coachbuilt with crew cab) and MkVI (based on an HCPU body). All were on the Defender 110 chassis.
Fish Conservation Transporters	were an unusual conversion, based on the 130 6x6 chassis with a dropside body arranged to carry tanks.
Lifestyle Vehicles	came in the shape of the 90SV, which is described further in Chapter 4.
Mobile Catering Units	were based on the 130 chassis with Quadtec high-roof body and had a raised centre roof section; they had three-man cabs.
Mobile Work Platforms	were available with a 10-metre working height on the 110 pick-up or HCPU, and with a 10-metre or 14-metre working height on the 130 chassis.

This Defender 130 by Special Vehicles carries a hydraulic work platform.

Police Communications Vehicles	on the 130 chassis had the Quadtec 4 high-roof box body and a three-man cab.
Tippers	came on the 130 chassis, with either three-man or crew cabs.
Valeting Vehicles	with high-pressure cleaning equipment on board were offered on the 110 pick-up, which then had a three-quarter tilt with side windows.
Workshops	could be built into the 110 hardtop, and there were several different types on the 130 chassis. Crew cab types came with either the Quadtec 1 low-roof box body or the Quadtec 2 high-roof box body; in either case, the cab's rear door windows could be blanked out in Britain to avoid VAT. With the three-man cab there were the Quadtec 3 low-roof box body and the Quadtec 4 high-roof box body, the latter with a roof which could be raised. In addition, a Quadtec body was available on the 6x6 chassis with the V8 engine only.

The conversion specialists got to work early on the One Ten. This ambulance body for an overseas customer was built by Herbert Lomas in 1983.

The original crew cab configuration on the 127-inch chassis was still available by the time this Defender 130 was built for export in 1996. Note the windows in the soft-top – normally an export-only option. This example has the 300 Tdi engine.

The 127-inch wheelbase chassis was ideal as the basis of an ambulance. This example was bought by the Suffolk Ambulance Service in the mid-Eighties. Note the grille badge still reads 'Land Rover 110'.

This specially-equipped Defender 110 Station Wagon was built for the Angolan Police in 1996.

CHAPTER 6

Overseas variations
Land Rovers built abroad

The restrictions on trade operated by some countries have always caused headaches for Land Rover, because the company depends so heavily on exporting its products. Most commonly, a government imposes heavy taxation on foreign-made vehicles entering its country in order to provide a degree of protection for local manufacturers; and sometimes, that taxation is so high as to make sales of imported vehicles impossible.

Nevertheless, the major motor manufacturers usually manage to find ways around this problem if they are keen enough to sell their vehicles in a particular country. Favourite methods have always been to establish manufacturing plants in the countries which tax imports or, where the cost of this is too high in relation to the likely benefits, to establish assembly plants and to ship kits of parts to them from the mother factory. In either case, the operation provides work for the local workforce; the assembly operations may also use locally-manufactured items to supplement those shipped from the mother factory, thus providing a further boost for the local economy.

Land Rovers have been assembled overseas since 1950, primarily from CKD (Completely Knocked Down) kits sent out from Solihull. In a few cases, such as the MSA (Santana) operation in Spain, the degree of local content has gradually increased until the whole vehicle is actually built in-territory. Over the years, the locations of these plants have changed in order to meet both changing political situations and Land Rover's own policies, and their number has shrunk considerably from the peak of more

than two dozen which it reached in the Sixties. However, several plants were still assembling Land Rovers during the Eighties and Nineties – the period of the coil-sprung models. In 1995, there were seven plants active – in Australia, Kenya, Malaysia, Morocco, South Africa, Turkey and Zimbabwe. Most of these produced just a few hundred Defender One Tens each year, and only the Malaysian plant at Selangor also turned out Defender 90s. However, three of them – in Australia, South Africa and Turkey – were rather larger operations.

Clearly, the scale on which these larger overseas assembly plants operate makes it economically viable for them to design and build quite significant variations from the standard Solihull build specification if their markets demand it. Even the smaller plants have sometimes been obliged to modify certain aspects of the basic specification – lighting arrangements, for example – and often items such as glass, tyres and paint have been sourced locally, but only the larger ones can go in for large-scale re-engineering. All three of Land Rover's major overseas plants have done so, following the lead of earlier (but now defunct) large operations such as the Belgian Minerva and Spanish Santana ones.

Australia
Land Rover's Australian arm has been responsible for a number of fascinating variants of the coil-sprung models, and those variants have embraced unique engines, bodywork, and chassis configurations and wheelbase

lengths. Even the models which look standard in fact have some interesting differences from the regular line-built Solihull product.

The One Ten was announced for the Australian market in November 1984, initially only in County Station Wagon form. Both petrol and diesel variants were offered, the petrol models having the 3.5-litre V8 engine and being shipped out from Solihull as complete vehicles. The diesel models, however, were assembled at Jaguar-Rover Australia's Moorebank plant in Sydney from CKD kits, and were fitted with an engine which has never been available in any Land Rover outside Australia.

These County Station Wagons all had 10 seats (rather than the 12 standard in Britain for tax reasons) and came with air conditioning as standard and with an anti-roll bar on the rear axle – a feature not available anywhere else. Even the V8 engine was not the same as that fitted to other One Tens, being in Range Rover tune with a 9.35:1 compression ratio and 125bhp at 4,000rpm; other One Ten V8s then had an 8.13:1 compression ratio and 114bhp. It

appears that Land Rover had fitted this version of the engine because it had already been homologated under the Australian exhaust emissions regulations, and to homologate the low-compression engine as well would have demanded both money and time.

The Isuzu diesel engine

The diesel engine was a big 3.9-litre direct-injection four-cylinder built by the Japanese Isuzu company and known as the 4BD1. JRA had been fitting it to long-wheelbase Land Rovers since 1981, when Solihull's inability to provide the powerful diesel engine JRA needed to make Land Rovers competitive with Toyota products drove the Australians to go their own way. The engine offered 97bhp at 3,200rpm – about 50% more than the four-cylinder Land Rover diesel of the time could manage – and had prodigious amounts of torque, its peak of 188lb.ft being delivered at just 1,900rpm. Despite a distinct lack of refinement, the 4BD1 certainly helped One Ten sales in Australia, not least because it brought fuel economy of around 25mpg as

The Isuzu 3.9-litre diesel engine was another feature unique to Australian-built coil-sprung Land Rovers.

Unique to Australia, and assembled there, was the 120-inch chassis. This example is fitted with the characteristic Australian 'tray top' and aftermarket eight-spoke wheels. The '3.9D' decal just visible behind the front wheelarch is a reminder that this – like all 120s – has the Isuzu diesel engine.

The massive load area of the 120 tray top.

opposed to the 16mpg which was normal with the petrol V8. One Tens with it were known as 3.9D models and wore appropriate decal badging behind their front wheelarches.

The 120 tray top
The reason why JRA offered only passenger-carrying One Tens at first was that it was developing its own load-carrier to meet conditions peculiar to Australia. This model was announced in March 1985, and came as a chassis/cab for the fitting of locally built bodywork. Sitting on a wheelbase of 119.6 inches (3,040mm), it had a One Ten chassis which had been stretched at the Moorebank plant by the simple insertion of extra sections in the chassis side rails and the addition of a longer propshaft. For longevity, the chassis was galvanized; and heavy-duty suspension components gave the vehicle a payload of 1.3 tonnes – the same as the One Ten HCPU sold in other markets. Unlike the Australian Station Wagons, however, the new model did not have an anti-roll bar on its rear axle.

To JRA, this vehicle was still a Land Rover One Ten, and more particularly a One Ten Heavy Duty model. The customers usually called it a 120, however, and that name stuck. It was available only with the Isuzu diesel engine, which appears to have come in slightly different tune from the version in the Station Wagons in order to give more low-speed pulling power for the heavier 120.

The 120 was normally finished in white, although some examples were probably painted in different colours to special order. The favourite body, which was available through JRA, was a shallow-sided dropside lorry known as a 'tray top', which was ideally suited to the Australian market. The tray was made of aluminium alloy (supplied by Alcan) and offered a load area 98.4 inches (2.5m) long and 78.7 inches (2m) wide. The extra wheelbase length helped to reduce the rear overhang common to this type of body and therefore to improve the vehicle's rough-terrain ability.

The Land Rover Dual Cab
By the end of 1985, Australian One Ten V8s had the five-speed LT85 Santana-built gearbox, and this was also fitted to the diesel-powered models from January or February 1986. Then, during 1986, the V8 engine was uprated to the same 134bhp tune as was found in Land Rovers for other markets. The Ninety was never put on sale in Australia, and the One Ten County and 120 chassis/cab models remained the only Land Rovers available in that market until June 1987, when JRA announced what it called the Land Rover Dual Cab or 110 County Pick-Up (the Australian company preferred the figures 110 to the One Ten name in words by this stage).

The Dual Cab was a strange hybrid which consisted of a four-door crew cab constructed mainly from Station Wagon parts, together with a shortened pick-up back body. Unlike SVO's Crew Cab model on the 127-inch wheelbase, however, the rear of the cab had a flat panel (presumably to save space) and the pick-up body was the standard type rather than a derivative of the HCPU. Either petrol V8 or Isuzu diesel engines could be had. However, few Dual Cabs were made: the vehicle appears to have been designed

The rear chassis of the Australian-built 6x6 Land Rover had a unique construction of galvanized steel tubing. The rear suspension was by semi-elliptic springs.

Civilian versions of the Australian 6x6 were used for special conversions such as this fire tender, which belongs to the National Parks and Wildlife Service and has an Isuzu turbocharged diesel engine.

originally for the Australian Bicentennial Authority, which took a batch, but the only dealer which sold examples to the public was Winterfaulls of Perth.

The Heavy-Duty 6x6

From 1986, Australian Land Rover buyers were also offered another new model not available elsewhere. This was a 6x6 model with a two-tonne payload, originally developed by JRA to meet Australian military requirements, and it was known as the One Ten Heavy-Duty 6x6. The story of the its military applications is told in Chapter 7.

Nothing Solihull had in its range could handle the two-tonne payload which was fundamental to the Australian military requirement, and even the 6x6 conversion available through SVO was not up to the task. So the JRA engineers decided to develop their own vehicle, beginning work in 1982 – before the One Ten was available and a good two years before it reached Australia. From the beginning, it was intended to be a three-axle six-wheeler with permanent four-wheel drive and selectable drive to the third axle. All

the development was done in Australia, although Solihull funded the project, set up the test parameters, provided specialist design assistance and supplied special components. The project was led by Ray Habgood, JRA's Land Rover engineering and product planning manager, and prototypes (which used Stage 1 V8 front end panels) were ready in time for the Australian Army trials in October 1983.

JRA had extended the rear chassis and fitted a third axle; the distance between the first and second axles was the same 119.6in (3,040mm) as on the 120-inch model. However, the whole chassis was actually quite different from the One Ten's, with deeper sidemembers and crossmembers at the front, and a fabricated section at the rear built up from square tube and channel-section steel. After completion, the whole frame was hot-dip galvanized.

Several different rear suspension layouts were tried during development, but JRA finally settled on a twin-axle bogie arrangement, with semi-elliptic springs on each axle linked by a load-sharing rocker beam. This gave excellent axle articulation for rough-terrain work, together with good resistance to body roll on the road. The two-tonne payload persuaded JRA to fit disc brakes to all six wheels, and both 15-inch and 16-inch wheel sizes were made available. Drive was provided through an LT95A gearbox, the latest version of the old Range Rover four-speed. Both front and second axles were permanently driven, and drive to the third axle was automatically engaged when the centre differential was locked; the third propshaft was driven from the centre power take-off on the transfer box.

As far as engines were concerned, the 3.5-litre V8 was powerful enough to haul this large vehicle around at respectable speeds, but JRA had their doubts about the Isuzu diesel. For the military versions of the 6x6, they turned instead to a turbocharged edition of the same engine, known as the 4BD1T and giving 115bhp and a massive 235lb.ft of torque at 1,800rpm. So although all three engines were eventually offered on the civilian 6x6, the turbodiesel was the one which became most closely associated with the model.

South Africa

The company responsible for assembling the coil-sprung Land Rovers in South Africa between 1985 and 1995 was AAD, which had bought out the Leyland South Africa interests during 1984. Assembly of One Tens from CKD kits was carried out at a plant in Cape Town, which had the capacity to build 800 vehicles a year.

The AAD plant was not equipped to handle small-run or one-off Land Rover conversions, but Land Rover's marketing people had identified a demand in South Africa which could be met by their 6x6 conversion. With import tax on a fully-built vehicle running at 100% (a measure adopted earlier to stem the tide of Japanese imports), it was clearly out of the question to consider shipping complete vehicles out from Solihull. So Land Rover reached a compromise, arranging for the conversions to be carried out in South Africa by local specialists on vehicles built or partly built by AAD. The contract for the 6x6 conversions went to the Safari Centre in Bryanston, Johannesburg.

Around 40 such conversions were done between 1986 and

A specialist South African conversion by the Safari Centre was this game-viewing vehicle on a 127-inch chassis.

1992, when the contract for their assembly was moved to AAD. However, it seems unlikely that AAD actually built any 6x6 conversions. All the 6x6s built by the Safari Centre had V8 engines and were mostly converted from One Ten chassis, although a small number of conversions were also done on the 127. These included a 16-seat Station Wagon for a safari company in Zimbabwe, two fire tenders and a trio of overhead cable inspection vehicles for the Eskom electricity supply company.

Even the pick-up body on the basic South African 6x6 conversion differed from Solihull's products, and the Safari Centre built both this and a variety of other intriguing bodies not seen elsewhere. Among these was an armour-plated van delivered to a diamond mining company. However, the biggest customer for the 6x6 conversion was the military of a neighbouring state, which took a total of 25 One Ten-based vehicles between 1988 and 1991. Some allegedly went to the military police, while others went to the army. Gun tractors with soft-top bodies and side-benches were the most numerous, accounting for 22 of the vehicles; one was a support vehicle for diving teams involved in rescue operations from swamps; and two were mobile command posts with caravan bodies. These towed a trailer with a generator to run their air conditioning units.

After BMW's acquisition of the Rover Group early in 1994, the Land Rover assembly agreement with AAD was an early casualty. Work began on a dedicated Land Rover assembly plant at Rosslyn, near the South African capital of Pretoria, where BMW had been running its own assembly operation since 1977. With the changed political outlook in the country after Nelson Mandela's election to the Presidency, things moved on quickly, and Her Majesty the Queen opened the new Land Rover assembly plant on March 24, 1995.

The Rosslyn plant has the capacity to build 2,500 Defenders a year from CKD kits, together with 620 Discoverys (initially shipped out in part-assembled form). This makes it potentially the biggest of all Land Rover's overseas CKD assembly operations. The first vehicles off the lines were Defender 110 pick-ups and Station Wagons, all painted white but with a choice of V8 or 300Tdi engines;

Defender 90s and other paint options followed in the autumn of 1995. The plant has pioneered assembly techniques different from those used at Solihull, mainly because of its smaller capacity. There is no moving assembly line, so vehicles are pushed from stage to stage of the assembly process on their own wheels; and the bulkheads and front wings are pre-assembled as a unit alongside the lines instead of being built up on the vehicles. In due course, the South African plant is expected to export a proportion of its vehicles to Sub-Saharan Africa and to Australia.

Turkey
Otokar was already well-established as the manufacturer of minibuses for the Turkish market when Land Rover established a CKD assembly operation at its Istanbul plant in 1987. The catalyst was an order for 400 soft-top and Station Wagon One Tens placed by the Jandarma – a paramilitary force combining the roles of police and certain other emergency services. So well received were these first vehicles that a further order for Ninety and One Ten models followed, and since then the plant has been busily supplying batches of Land Rovers regularly to the Jandarma. Its annual capacity is about 2,000 vehicles, and about 75% of all those built go to military or paramilitary customers. The remaining 25% go mostly to Turkish Government and public service users or to civil contractors, typical examples being the Ministry of Health and Social Assistance, the Public Telecommunications Company, Turkish Petroleum and the Minerals Research Institute.

The Land Rovers built by Otokar are distinguished by rectangular Otokar badges behind each front wheelarch, and all wear pre-Defender style grille badges – probably because the Turks find the Defender name too hard to pronounce! All three wheelbase varieties are produced, and the high percentage of local content includes the chassis frames which are pressed and welded in Istanbul. Engines, transmissions and shaped body panels, however, come from Solihull, the latter ensuring that at least the basic soft-top, hardtop and Station Wagon variants closely resemble the standard Land Rover types. Nevertheless, there are special

This One Ten breakdown truck is operated by the Turkish Jandarma paramilitary police, and was built in Istanbul by Otokar.

Not assembled abroad, but modified by the importers to suit local tastes: this is a French-market Ninety, and shows the special graphics used in that market.

features on these, One Ten Station Wagons for example having a two-piece rear bumper and a swingaway spare-wheel carrier on the rear panel.

Otokar has its own design and development team, which works closely with Solihull's engineers on special variants to meet local needs, and several unique body styles have been built in Istanbul. These have included ambulances, recovery vehicles, mobile laboratories and military personnel carriers, the latter on both the 110-inch and 127-inch wheelbases and featuring high-line tilts. In addition, Otokar builds its own design of armoured car and armoured personnel carrier, both on strengthened versions of the One Ten chassis.

In the later Nineties, Otokar hopes to move to a new and much larger site where it will be able to expand its Land

Rover assembly operation to meet export orders. The early part of the decade saw Otokar Land Rovers on trial with the Pakistani military, and the company had by then identified a number of export markets to tackle, among them markets denied to Solihull's own vehicles on political grounds.

Special French graphics again: this is a late-model Ninety Diesel Turbo ('Turbo D' in France). The French importers considered it necessary to remind onlookers that the vehicle has permanent four-wheel drive!

The special bodywork on this Tdi-powered Defender 130 was actually built in the UK, but the vehicle was specifically designed for use as a tour bus in Kenya and has four rows of seats.

CHAPTER 7

At peace and at war

Military Land Rovers

Someone once estimated that around 40% of all the Land Rovers ever built have entered service with military or paramilitary organizations. Indeed, that factor was a major influence on the choice of the Defender name for the coil-sprung models of the Nineties – a period when the military Land Rover remained as popular as ever. Solihull's military sales team was constantly seeking new customers and with considerable success, but in many cases the vehicle sold itself. Thus, during the Gulf War in 1991, when the British elements of the coalition forces deployed Land Rovers in huge quantities, the American military were so impressed by the qualities of the vehicles they saw that they ordered a batch for their own elite US Rangers. Civilian sales of Land Rovers followed in the USA quickly after that....

Land Rover had One Ten military demonstrators ready shortly after the new model went on sale to the public in 1983, but the first deliveries of military variants were not made until 1985. That time-lapse did not reflect any problems with the vehicle; it is simply that military fleet-buyers take a long time to make up their minds, generally evaluating a group of competitive vehicles in demanding trials until one emerges as the best suited to their requirements. There was also the fact that Solihull still had large military fleet orders for the Series III models to fulfil when the One Ten was announced, and it would not have looked good to be delivering the older vehicles to customers after the improved new ones had become available!

In fact, the British Ministry of Defence ordered One Tens as part of its rolling programme of vehicle replacement at a very early stage, and the first order from an overseas customer came from the Netherlands as early as 1984. The military One Ten was soon supplemented by a military version of the Ninety, and in due course Solihull was also able to promote the 127-inch Land Rover as a military model as well. All three types were well-liked by procurement agencies and – perhaps more important – by the soldiers in the field whose livings and often lives depended on them. Their common mechanical basis also offered considerable logistical advantages, by minimizing both training requirements and the quantity and variety of spares which a fighting unit needed to carry in the field. By the time the Defender came on-stream in the Nineties, the coil-sprung Land Rovers had earned themselves a formidable reputation as war – or, more commonly, peace-keeping – machines.

Probably the vast majority of military coil-sprung Land Rovers have been and always will be soft-top One Ten General Service types, suitable for carrying troops or cargo (and often both at once) and for towing small trailers and light guns. However, Solihull and its overseas assembly plants have always been sensitive to the specific requirements of military customers, because the cost of developing a special body or specially-equipped vehicle may be repaid many times over if a large fleet order follows. The creation of bespoke military Land Rovers has also attracted speculative ventures by military equipment specialists outside Land Rover, and the Nineties in particular have seen an exciting and bewildering array of different Land

The Ninety has always been less common in military service than its long-wheelbase contemporaries. This British Army hardtop was pictured on exercises in Canada, and is a 24-volt FFR (Fitted For Radio) model. The front bumper carries the characteristic towing pintle and the sidelights and indicators are the standard waterproofed military type.

Rover-based military specials. Unfortunately, it is often not possible to discover how many (if any) of such conversions have been sold, as their creators are reluctant to divulge details of end-users and equally reluctant to admit that their designs have been commercial failures.

The great variety of military coil-sprung models created by bodywork and other specialist adaptations is increased even further by the different engine and transmission combinations which have been supplied over the years. Every engine ever available on the civilian market in a coil-sprung Land Rover has also found its way at one time or another into a military model – and that means a lot of different engines. The three original engines (2.3-litre petrol and diesel, petrol V8) have been supplemented by two enlarged four-cylinders (the 2.5-litre petrol and diesel types), by the Diesel Turbo, and latterly by the 200Tdi and 300Tdi turbodiesels. That alone makes eight different engines, without counting variations in detail specification, engines available only in certain countries (like the Isuzu diesels in Australian military models), and engines which

Solihull is unwilling to talk about!

The military Ninety and Defender 90
The short-wheelbase coil-sprung Land Rover has always been the least common in military service, and for some very good reasons. Principal among these is that its relatively restricted load-carrying ability makes it less versatile than larger vehicles, a problem for which even its greater agility cannot compensate. In many military forces, it was called upon to replace the 88-inch wheelbase Land Rover runabouts used for rear echelon and support duties, but relatively few customers wanted Ninetys to replace their Lightweight (Half-Tonne) Land Rovers. With bigger transport aircraft and the greater lifting power of the latest heavy helicopters, many forces saw the One Ten as a far preferable Lightweight replacement.

However, the Ninety certainly has found military customers, and examples have been delivered with both the standard 12-volt electrical system and with the 24-volt FFR (Fitted For Radio) specification. Ninetys have often been

This very early military One Ten was pictured at Solihull in May 1983 and was probably a trials vehicle for the British Army. Note the jerrycan stowage hatch ahead of the rear wheel, the dual fuel fillers for the twin fuel tanks, the bumperettes at the rear and the radio mast supports alongside the tilt.

specified for communications and liaison duties rather than as cargo or personnel carriers, and for that reason the most common military Ninety is a hardtop. Soft-tops have also been ordered, however, and are popular with units for whom space in transport aircraft or sea craft is a major consideration. Thus, the soft-top Ninety has often been found in service with airborne, airmobile and amphibious military units. In the early Nineties, Solihull introduced its MRCV (Multi-Role Combat Vehicle) conversion on the Defender 90 as well as on Defender 110 and 130 chassis. Among the other characteristics of this versatile vehicle were a full rollcage over the door-less driving compartment, and a weapons' ring mount integrated into a rearward extension of that rollcage, with provision for ammunition stowage in cages above the rear wheels.

Some of the best-known – though least numerous – military Ninetys were the diesel models acquired by the British SAS during the Gulf War in 1991. With all the Regiment's One Ten desert patrol vehicles engaged behind enemy lines, something was needed to escort the resupply convoys, and these Ninetys were all that was available in a hurry. Converted into miniature versions of the 'Pink Panther' or 'Pinky' One Ten (so called after the pink desert camouflage of the original Series IIA 109 versions), they quickly acquired the nickname of 'Dinkies', which probably did more than anything else to ensure their fame when they returned home after the war!

The military One Ten and Defender 110
The 110-inch wheelbase coil-sprung Land Rover has been Solihull's core military product since the first half of the Eighties, and versions of it have also been assembled at overseas plants. The most common type is undoubtedly the GS soft-top, but hardtop and Station Wagon vehicles have also entered military service in various parts of the world, and the vehicle is also found with a variety of special configurations. Some of these are unit conversions rather than factory-produced, such as the TANGI armoured One Ten hardtops used by the Royal Ulster Constabulary during the Troubles in Northern Ireland.

The Shorland Series 5 armoured car based on the V8-powered One Ten chassis could trace its ancestry back to the first armoured cars built for counter-insurgency work in the Sixties.

Glover Webb also built an armoured car on the One Ten chassis. Theirs was called the Hornet.

The One Ten qualifies as being the vehicle which introduced the diesel-engined Land Rover to the British armed forces (although a few diesel vehicles had been procured earlier for special tasks). Starting with the first deliveries of One Tens in 1985, diesel power became standard on the British military Land Rover, and it was therefore unfortunate that some of these first deliveries should have been afflicted with engine problems – caused by a combination of faulty manufacture and the troops' unfamiliarity with diesel engines – within a couple of years of their delivery. Solihull, of course, rectified all the problems under warranty, and the British military remained one of scores of faithful One Ten fleet customers all over the world.

Once a decision had been taken that the Stage 2 Land Rovers should have wheelbases of 110 inches and 92.9 inches, a GS version of the One Ten was the first new military variant which Solihull developed. In standard specification, this can be recognized by its characteristic jerrycan hatch ahead of the rear wheelarch and by its double-bumper (actually double quarter-bumpers) at the front. However, not every soft-top One Ten in military service has the standard military specification; in Eire, for example, the Permanent Defence Force often buys civilian-specification vehicles through Land Rover dealers and then modifies them in its own workshops to suit its requirements.

Meanwhile, Short Brothers of Belfast were busily adapting their proven Shorland armoured car design to the One Ten V8 chassis. First seen in the mid-Sixties on the Series IIA 109-inch Land Rover, this design found users all over the world, particularly in developing countries; in One Ten

The Land Rover Special Operations Vehicle was designed in conjunction with the US Rangers and built specially for them.

During the Gulf War, a need for convoy escort vehicles arose when the SAS Regiment's Land Rover 110 Desert Patrol Vehicles were all committed on operations. As a result, a small number of diesel-powered Ninetys were converted to do the job. They were known as 'Dinkies' (small diesel-powered editions of the larger 'Pinkies' or 'Pink Panther' 110s)!

guise, it was known as a Shorland Series V. The same company also developed an armoured personnel carrier from its earlier SB401 on the One Ten chassis during the Eighties, as well as the SB505 anti-hijack armoured vehicle. All these vehicles had very distinctive armoured bodies.

By the mid-Eighties, several new and more specialized versions of the military One Ten were under development, and the first of these to enter service was the Desert Patrol Vehicle (DPV), prepared by Solihull in conjunction with Marshall's of Cambridge as a replacement for the British SAS 'Pink Panther' Land Rovers. Essentially a stripped-down One Ten HCPU with heavy-duty suspension, the DPV also featured long-range fuel tanks and a rollover bar behind the driving compartment. Smoke dischargers front and rear were standard equipment, and various different weapon mounts could be fitted – typically one GPMG (General Purpose Machine Gun) on a swivel mount in the load area and a second on the front bulkhead. The DPVs were also bought by some overseas countries.

Also developed by Solihull was the Special Operations

Vehicle (SOV), initially prepared for the US Rangers and announced at the Eurosatory Exhibition in Paris in 1992 before entering service in 1993. The Defender SOV was essentially a V8-powered One Ten chassis equipped as an airportable mobile gunship for rapid intervention work. Distinctive features included a rigid weapons mount incorporated as part of the rollover cage which covered the rear of the vehicle, and cutaway rear body sides ahead of the wheelarches to allow rapid crew deployment.

The Nineties also saw Solihull introduce MRCV versions of the One Ten, which will doubtless find customers as time goes on. Other interesting military models based on the One Ten have been produced by military vehicle specialists. The Glover Webb RAPV (Remote Area Patrol Vehicle), a vehicle similar to Solihull's own DPV which has found customers in the Middle East, saw service with peacekeeping forces in Bosnia in the first half of the decade. Meanwhile, the Courtaulds CAV100, which is essentially a van-bodied One Ten wearing S-2 Glass composite plastic armour, also saw service in Bosnia and was employed in

This One Ten, built for an unspecified overseas military force, shows a typical weapons fit in the load bed.

Military requirements prompted the most ingenious schemes. This is a demountable POD ambulance body, fitted to a One Ten pick-up. The vehicle dates from the late Eighties.

Northern Ireland before the ceasefire.

The military 127 and Defender 130

Largest of the core military Land Rovers was the 127-inch model, later rechristened Defender 130. Its size has permitted a wide variety of configurations, many of them also making use of its additional payload – at 1,600kg, some 25% more than that of a One Ten. However, the most popular military uses of this vehicle have been as ambulances and light artillery tractors.

The British military, for example, has taken ambulances with bodies by Marshall's and by Locomotors, for use both as battlefield ambulances and as airfield ambulances. Other military authorities have taken similar vehicles. In soft-top form, usually with high-line tilts and rear bodies by Marshall's, the 127 and Defender 130 are commonly seen towing Rapier missile units.

Australian military Land Rovers

Among the most interesting of the special military Land

Rovers built overseas have been those constructed for the Australian Army by Jaguar-Rover Australia (JRA). It was in 1982 that the Australian Army announced Project Perentie – the quest for a fleet of 3,000 all-terrain vehicles to replace those which were then in service. Of those 3,000 vehicles, 2,600 were to be one-tonne types to replace the Army's existing Series III 109-inch Land Rovers. JRA, with Solihull's support, was keen to keep the Land Rover flag flying, and therefore determined to bid for that contract.

The Australian Army wanted diesel power, and so the Isuzu engine used in Australian-built civilian Land Rovers was a logical choice for JRA's contender. In addition, the Army did not want the spare wheel inside the vehicle's body or on its bonnet, and so the One Ten's rear chassis was splayed so that the wheel could be carried under the tail. In consequence, the fuel tank had to be relocated further forward. Of course, further special features were incorporated to meet military requirements.

The JRA One Ten was one of seven vehicles put forward to tender for the contract, a number which had been

The Perentie contract for the Australian military was an important one to Land Rover, and the vehicles which fulfilled it were all built in Australia. This is the basic Perentie One Ten. Note the absence of a front bumper, the solid-looking bush-bar and the winch.

The Perentie contract also called for large load-carriers, and Land Rover supplied a version of the Australian-built 6x6, with a specially widened cab. This is a standard cargo truck version.

Most spectacular of the Perentie vehicles was undoubtedly the 6x6 Desert Patrol Vehicle, which was later offered through the UK company to other military users. The light motorcycle carried at the rear was standard equipment on the Australian vehicle.

whittled down to three by May 1983, when the Army ordered examples of each vehicle for trials. The trials began in September, with three vehicles from each of the contending manufacturers. Two of each type were tested by the Light Truck Trials Team at Puckapunyal, while the third was assessed by the Army's Engineering Development Establishment at Monegeetta, Victoria. Much to the delight of both JRA and Solihull, the Land Rover effort was rewarded with the contract for all 2,600 vehicles some three years later. The Army announced its intentions in July 1986, the contract was formally signed in October, and the first of the new vehicles was completed at the Moorebank plant early in 1987. The initial batch of Perentie One Tens was accepted into service in August that year. Production continued at the rate of some 350 vehicles a year, and the final One Tens ordered under that original contract reached

the Australian Army in 1994.

Six different versions of the Perentie One Ten were delivered during that time. The basic vehicle was a General Service soft-top; this was supplemented by an FFR soft-top and by a soft-top 'surveillance' vehicle. There were also three closed-body types, all distinguished by safari roofs (which were never available on other One Tens). These were a hardtop radio truck, a Station Wagon, and an FFR Station Wagon intended for senior commanders.

The second Australian military vehicle was developed to meet the Army's requirement for a vehicle in the 1.5 to 2-tonne payload class, and for this JRA drew up the 6x6 chassis with its Isuzu turbodiesel engine already described in Chapter 6. However, the military versions had a number of differences from the 6x6 which was made available on the civilian market in 1986. The military 6x6's front axle was a wide-track version of the One Ten's, strengthened by means of stiffening tubes pressed inside its housing and fitted with a stronger four-pinion differential. Constant-rate coil springs were used in place of the One Ten's dual-rate type, and lifted the ride height of the front end by 25mm (just under an inch). At the rear, both axles were wide-track versions of the One Ten's Salisbury 8HA fully-floating type, with strengthened casings and long-travel dampers developed specially for the 6x6 by Monroe-Wylie. Even the wheels were specially developed, looking like the standard items but actually being thicker in the nave area.

The military 6x6 was designed to carry different body modules, so that the basic vehicle could be converted in the field from 12-seat troop carrier to Rapier tractor, ambulance, field maintenance truck or electronic

One that got away: the forward-control Llama. This is number LFC 008, the only example which used a diesel (actually Diesel Turbo) engine, and was trialled by the British Army as a replacement for the Land Rover 101 Forward Control.

equipment maintenance truck. The canvas top, hood sticks and longitudinal seats in the load bed of the basic vehicle could all be removed and stowed below the tray, and an alternative body module could simply be lifted into place and bolted down. There was also a special version of the 6x6, designed as a long-range patrol vehicle for the Australian SAS.

The Perentie 6x6 was opposed by only one vehicle from another manufacturer, and the announcement that it had been awarded the contract was made at the same time as the announcement about the Perentie One Ten's success. However, there was one condition which seems to have been imposed at the eleventh hour: the Australian Army insisted that the closed-cab versions should come with an enlarged cab – and the prototype of that cab was under construction in JRA's workshops shortly after the announcement was made.

The 'wide cab' which went into production was essentially a standard Land Rover cab widened by 200mm (7.8in), lengthened by around 2.5 inches and with its roof raised by around 2 inches to give additional headroom. In addition, it had a deeper rear window to improve rearward visibility. On early examples, a standard One Ten facia panel was used, and the extra space at either end was filled with stowage clips for rifles; later models had a unique new dashboard moulding. A new bonnet panel also had to be designed, and JRA made that up from GRP with a welded steel supporting structure.

The JRA 6x6 was offered to other military users from May 1989, and Solihull brought three examples to Britain to act as demonstrators. Whether any found homes with military users outside Australia is unclear at present.

The ill-fated Llama
By the mid-Eighties, the British military was beginning to think about the vehicles it would eventually need to replace its forward-control Land Rover 101 One-tonnes, which had served faithfully as gun tractors and in a variety of other roles since the mid-Seventies. When it invited tenders to meet the latest requirement, Land Rover determined to put in a bid.

The vehicle which Solihull developed was a new forward-control type based on One Ten V8 running-gear and known as Project Llama. The Llama had a steel-framed GRP cab which pivoted forward on a triangular extension at the front of its modified One Ten chassis to give access to the engine. With a 2-tonne payload, a high percentage of common parts with the existing production vehicles, and the possibility of civilian sales as well, it deserved success.

Two Llama prototypes were supplied for trials to RARDE, the British military vehicle test authority, in February 1986. Initial examination showed that the vehicles did not meet the Army's tilt and stability criteria, and so one of them was returned to Solihull for modifications. When it returned to RARDE in April, there was insufficient time to put it though a full test cycle. Even so, the test authority did not like what it saw, and its tests appear to have revealed a number of design flaws which were considered fundamental. Solihull, meanwhile, was confident enough of success to display a Llama at the British Army Equipment Exhibition in June – not knowing that RARDE had already filed the report which spelled the end of its chances with the British military. In addition, Land Rover did a trial build of one Llama on the production lines, in anticipation of putting the vehicle into production.

It was not to be. Despite a last-ditch attempt to curry favour with a Llama Diesel Turbo, Solihull was forced to concede defeat and the military contract went to the Reynolds Boughton RB44 – a vehicle which has been so unpopular with the soldiers who have to use it that many units have preferred to retain their elderly Land Rover 101s. Whether any overseas military authorities showed interest in the Llama when it was exhibited in June 1986 is not clear, but by the end of the year, Land Rover had decided not to commit the vehicle to production. Several prototypes still survive, in the Heritage Collection at Gaydon and in the hands of the Dunsfold Land Rover Trust.

The Defender XD range
The early Nineties saw the British armed forces conducting trials to find a new generation of 4x4 vehicles to enter service at the end of the decade and through into the 21st century. Four categories of vehicle were specified – TUL (Truck, Utility, Light), TUM (Truck, Utility, Medium), TUM (HD) (Truck, Utility, Medium, Heavy Duty), and a battlefied ambulance – and Solihull resolved to field a contender in each class.

The new military Land Rovers were developed under the project code of Wolf, and a first batch of trials vehicles was supplied in 1993. Battlefield trials showed up weaknesses in the bodywork of these, and so Solihull strengthened the structure and submitted modified 'Wolf 2' vehicles. These were successful in three of the four categories – the TUM (HD) contract was awarded to the Austrian-built Pinzgauer – and the official announcement of the contract was made in January 1996. In the meantime, Land Rover had introduced the Wolf 2 vehicles to a wider audience at the British Army Equipment Exhibition in September 1995. At that point, Wolf 2 became known as the Defender XD range, those letters standing for eXtra Duty.

Land Rover successfully bid for the British Army's TUL (Truck, Utility, Light) contract, which was awarded to the specially-developed Defender XD 90 in 1996. Note the shielded air intake behind the wheelarch, the high tilt and the optional side mounting for the spare wheel.

The tubular rollover bars which support the tilt can be clearly seen in this cutaway view of a Defender XD 110 24-volt hardtop.

The Defender XD 90, 110 and 130 models had been specifically designed as military vehicles and were intended as complementary to the existing Defenders. They also looked very much like the existing models, although there were two very distinctive features. The first was the louvered air intake box on each front wing behind the wheelarch, designed as a dust extractor for extreme conditions to protect the 300Tdi engine with which they were all fitted. The second was the spare-wheel mounting on the side of the vehicle just behind the cab on soft-top models: one wheel could thus be carried on each side, and a third on the bonnet if necessary.

However, the Defender XD models were actually very different from the standard Defenders in very many ways, their bodies and chassis having been extensively redeveloped to produce substantially more robust components. Stronger side rails and crossmembers had increased the structural strength of the frame, and the body was more rigidly mounted to the chassis by new integral side and rear structures. These also reinforced the body itself, which was further strengthened by a rollover bar above the cab area and a rollcage over the back body. Both these items could be removed for low-profile operations, of course.

Hardtop and soft-top bodies were both taller than on the standard Defender, partly to clear the rollover bars and partly to increase headroom in the rear body, where the bench seats were all provided with safety harnesses. Instead of the canvas used on British military vehicles, the soft-tops were made of a synthetic material which had been supplied to overseas military customers for a number of years. Land Rover described the body construction as 'modular', explaining that this made the fitting of other bodies simpler when necessary, and reassured potential customers that all existing equipment developed for the Defender could also be used on the Defender XD.

Despite the extra weight of these more robust bodies and chassis, the vehicles could carry up to 20% more payload than the standard Defenders, that of the XD 90 being up to 600kg and that of the XD 110 up to 1,200kg. Other drivetrain elements had, of course, been strengthened to cope: there were a stronger rear axle with a four-pinion differential, special heavy-duty wheels with distinctive perforated rims, and, of course, the latest R380 primary gearbox. Like the latest standard Defenders, the XD models had disc brakes all round.

Among the vehicles announced in September 1995 was also a new military ambulance on the Defender XD 130 chassis, developed in conjunction with Marshall's of Cambridge to meet a British military requirement. This was a four-stretcher type with gas struts to assist loading and unloading of the upper stretcher racks, and with a sophisticated range of lighting for the separately air-conditioned and heated rear body.

With such radically redeveloped models to take the range into the 21st century, it is clear that Solihull is committed to the Defender as a military vehicle for at least the foreseeable future. Time alone will tell how successful the latest XD range will be, but its introduction has silenced the rumours, rife towards the middle of the Nineties, that Defender production was soon to be scaled down to allow Solihull to concentrate on its upmarket Discovery, Range Rover and other forthcoming models.

CHAPTER 8

Motorsport and adventure

The other faces of Land Rover

There is a certain irony about the fact that the Stage 2 Land Rovers, arguably the most able off-road vehicles ever to come from Solihull, have predominantly sold to people who hardly ever make use of their rough-terrain abilities. The Ninetys and One Tens were born into a boom period for 4x4s, when the Japanese stampede to imitate and undercut the Range Rover aroused a great interest in the 4x4 as an alternative to the family estate. During the Eighties, the Land Rover Station Wagons became a chic mode of town transport, bringing with them the subtle hint that their drivers actually had a place in the country as well as a town house. As insurance premiums on the hot hatchbacks which had dominated the youth market went sky-high, so a Land Rover – preferably a soft-top for summer motoring – became one of the favoured replacements.

It is, of course, easy to sneer at those who buy a Land Rover for the image it promotes; but the fact is that Solihull itself has pandered to this trend ever since the mid-Eighties. It is also true that the growth of interest in 4x4 vehicles has been accompanied by a much smaller but still steady growth of interest in off-road driving. Increasing numbers of individuals in the civilized countries are finding that a 4x4 makes a fine recreational vehicle, and taking a 4x4 into the country at weekends has to some extent replaced the weekend trip to a racing circuit with the sportscar which was once so much a feature of the enthusiast motoring scene.

Of course, just as the terrain available for off-road driving differs from country to country, so do the regulations governing what 4x4 drivers may and may not do. In the USA, for example, there are vast tracts of country with long-established trails to explore; in Australia, the outback presents its own challenges; and in Britain, the pleasant pastime of green laning (driving through unspoilt countryside on clearly defined routes) is available. However, nothing gives the off-road fraternity a bad name as much as the irresponsible individuals who drive recklessly across country, spoiling the enjoyment of others who use the countryside and causing lasting environmental damage. Land Rover itself has for some years now operated a 'Fragile Earth' policy (its US equivalent is called 'Tread Lightly') which aims to promote responsible use of the countryside by those who drive off-road. For those who wish to discover the delights of off-road driving in the country, several clubs and organizations have grown up to give guidance and provide camaraderie. Their contact addresses can usually be found in the leading magazines devoted to off-road vehicles.

A lot of off-road driving is fairly undemanding, although drivers do need to understand the capabilities of their vehicles. However, Land Rovers are built to tackle the very worst conditions that Nature can provide, and many drivers want to see just what the vehicles can do. To cater for those who want to learn about more demanding off-road driving, dozens of off-road driving schools and off-road recreational centres have been established in Britain. Land Rover also runs its own, very professional, Land Rover Experience driving school, which is aimed at professional off-road

Off-road recreational driving does not call for heroics – quite the reverse, in fact. However, when tackling really difficult terrain, it is sensible to use a vehicle equipped with a winch for self-recovery. Note also the aggressive tread on the tyres of this Ninety – ideal for maximum traction in deep mud.

Shallow wading is no problem to a Land Rover One Ten...

...and there is a great deal of satisfaction to be had from driving through deep water like this without problems. Many drivers prefer diesel power for recreational off-road use, partly because diesel engines are less susceptible than petrol types to problems caused by water.

For all types of off-road driving, whether recreational or competitive, it is vital to understand what the vehicle can and cannot be expected to do. The best way of learning is to take a course with one of the recognized off-road schools. This Ninety – showing the impressive axle articulation which makes the coil-sprung Land Rovers such good off-road vehicles – belongs to David Bowyer's well-known off-road driving school in Devon.

drivers; there are also excellent instructional publications and videos available. It must be said that there is a great deal of satisfaction to be had from easing a vehicle over difficult terrain without causing damage. Sadly, as in all branches of recreational motoring, the amateur heroics of a minority of unskilled hoodlums will always be a blot on the landscape.

Trials

For well over 30 years now, Land Rover drivers have banded together in clubs to indulge their competitive instincts in off-road driving. A piece of land is hired for a weekend (or sometimes longer), a demanding course is laid out and various competitive events are organized. There are

several different types, ranging from RTV (Road Taxed Vehicle) trials best suited to those who bring along their everyday Land Rovers, to Comp Safari (Competition Safari) events designed for heavily-modified and specially built vehicles. All of them are closely governed by rules designed to ensure safety as well as fair play, and these rules are established and regularly reviewed by the Association of Rover Clubs in Britain and by equivalent bodies overseas.

Such events make excellent spectator sport as well as being fun for the participants. Even long-time Land Rover addicts admit to the thrill of watching one of Solihull's finest claw its way through axle-deep mud, haul its way out of a water-filled 'bomb hole', or power gently down a slippery slope while the driver remains in full control. For events like these, a Ninety or Defender 90 makes an ideal mount, as its short wheelbase, minimal front and rear overhangs, and huge axle articulation give it superb off-road abilities. What

counts here is the driver's skill and the engine torque: for that reason, a Tdi-powered Defender is as able as its equivalent with a petrol V8.

Long-distance events

Outside Britain – which is, after all, a relatively small and densely-populated country – there is far greater scope for long-distance off-road driving events. These proliferated in the Eighties, when 4x4 manufacturers recognized that success generated valuable publicity and did wonders for the image of a marque. Land Rover as a company has steered clear of such events, preferring instead to put its weight behind the Camel Trophy (see below), although Land Rover France has run its own off-road racing team since 1993 in the French Endurance Rally series. This series attracts works teams from all the major 4x4 manufacturers, and after using Range Rovers successfully

A Ninety Station Wagon scrabbles for grip on the steep slope leading out of a water-filled 'bomb hole' during an enthusiast's off-road event.

A winch is an essential item if you really intend to do some heavy off-roading.

for two years, the Rover France team switched to Defender 110s in 1995.

Even more gruelling than the French Endurance Rally series are the international long-distance rallies which also attract works teams. The vehicles which compete in these events, the most famous of which is probably the Paris-Dakar Rally, are very heavily modified and bear only a limited resemblance to their roadgoing equivalents. Land Rover has never seen any point in investing huge amounts of money to compete, as the potential benefits to Defender sales are minimal. Nevertheless, there have been coil-sprung Land Rovers in these long-distance rallies, their crews being heavily sponsored by big companies out to gain as much as possible from the wide TV coverage which the rallies get on the European continent.

In addition, there are a number of rather different European off-road events in which the coil-sprung Land Rovers can often be seen. These depend on the off-road driving skill of the driver and on the abilities of the vehicles rather than on the speed and durability which lead to success in long-distance rallies. They include the annual Warn Trophy (sponsored by the makers of the Warn winches which Solihull recommends) and the French *Mille Rivières*.

Adventure sport – the Camel Trophy

The organizers of the Camel Trophy event describe it as "The Ultimate Adventure", which is as good a description as any of this unique and spectacular annual convoy through inhospitable terrain. It also encapsulates what is so special about the Trophy – that it is not a race. True, it does contain an element of competition, as the vehicle crews strive to out-perform each other on a series of special tasks; but above all, the Camel Trophy combines adventure, skill and stamina in a way no other event has managed. Each crew is drawn from a different country, and that, of course, encourages further friendly rivalry. In recent years, the Camel Trophy has gone on to embrace tasks of environmental importance and to help local communities as it passes on its way.

Recognizing the benefits in terms of publicity and marque image, Land Rover became involved with the Trophy during its second year (1981), and more recently has become a joint sponsor with Worldwide Brands Inc, an associated company of the American makers of Camel cigarettes who were its original sole sponsors. Ever since 1981, Land Rover has provided the vehicles both for the crews and for the support teams which travel with the Camel Trophy convoy. Coil-sprung Land Rovers have regularly featured as recce and support vehicles on the Camel Trophy, and in the latter role the vast carrying capacity of the Land Rover 127 and Defender 130 have made them favourites. However, Solihull makes careful use of the Trophy to showcase its latest products, and the coil-sprung utilities have therefore not always been used as the crew vehicles.

However, before the Discovery took over as the regular Camel Trophy crew vehicle in 1990, coil-sprung Land Rover Station Wagons featured in no fewer than five Camel Trophy events. Diesel One Tens carried the crews on the 1984 event; diesel-engined Ninetys were used in 1985 and 1986; and Diesel Turbo One Tens were favoured for 1988 and 1989. The intervening event in 1987 was used to showcase the then-new Range Rover Turbo D. Diesel engines were used every year, mainly because their greater economy reduced the need to carry supplies of fuel and because they were less likely than petrol engines to suffer from water-induced malfunctions.

1984 – Brazil

By the time of the 1984 Camel Trophy, international interest in the event was running at a very high level, and the organizers had to cope with more than half a million applications from would-be participants. This year, the Trophy was held in the Amazon Basin, scene of the very first Camel Trophy back in 1980, and began at Manaus in Brazil where the earlier event had ended.

The timing of the event unfortunately did not marry up very well with Land Rover's new-model launches that year. The 2.5-litre diesel engine had replaced the older 2.3-litre type in January 1984, but there was insufficient time for SVO to prepare examples of the newer vehicles for the Trophy in early spring, and so the crews used One Tens with the superseded engine. This fact was glossed over when one of the 12 team vehicles was displayed on the Land Rover stand at the Birmingham Motor Show that autumn!

The 1984 event was in fact not one which those involved remember with particular fondness. It had been planned to start just after the rainy season had ended, but in practice the Amazon was still 69ft above its normal level when the convoy set out. As a result, the planned route would have been better suited to boats than to Land Rovers. The fall-back route was also next to impassable, being almost totally submerged in mud. Three times, the teams had to construct 40ft bridges to get their vehicles across flooded rivers, but the convoy did get through as a result of the determination of all its participants to succeed. The team prize of the Camel Trophy itself was awarded to the Italian crew of Alfredo Redaelli and Maurizio Levi.

1985 – Borneo

The rainy season was once again a factor on the 1985 Camel Trophy. For this year, the event was held on the island of Borneo, one of the world's least explored places. The rains slowed the convoy's progress across the mountainous East Kalimantan jungle region, and on some days it proved impossible to cover more than two or three kilometres. Things got so bad at one point that only an improvised helicopter lift – with the crew Ninetys being plucked individually out of the jungle – was able to keep the Trophy on the road.

This was not the sort of publicity Land Rover really wanted from the Camel Trophy, and no doubt there were some heated discussions about the future when the Trophy ended. The need for the helicopter rescue was in fact not the result of any failing in the Ninetys, nor indeed was it the fault of the crews. Land Rover put it down to organizational failings, and for the next year resolved that one of its own off-road driving experts should recce the route.

One very positive thing did come out of the 1985 event, however. The appalling conditions under which it was run brought out the very best in the crews, who worked together to ensure that the whole convoy got through to its destination. As a result, the organizers decided to present a second award alongside the Camel Trophy itself (which this year was won by the Germans Heinz Kallin and Bernd Strohdach): the Camel Trophy Team Spirit Award, presented to the team which had done most to ensure the overall success of the event. For 1985 it went to the Brazilian team of Tito Rosenberg and Carlos Probst. The Team Spirit Award has been an important feature of the Camel Trophy ever since.

1986 – Australia

There were some changes for 1986: not only did Land Rover provide its own Competitions Manager, Graham Fazakarley, to recce the proposed route, but the company

A diesel Ninety fording a river on the 1986 Camel Trophy event in Australia.

also insisted that a British team should be included for the first time. The official line had been that there was no publicity mileage to be made from the event in Britain because Camel cigarettes were not sold there. However, Land Rover argued that they wanted their fair share of publicity from the event, and that as Land Rovers *were* sold in Britain, there should be a British team.

It may well have been Land Rover which influenced the choice of Australia as the venue for the 1986 event. That was the year when the Australian Army was due to announce who had won the Perentie contract (see Chapter 7), and Solihull could no doubt see the benefit of the publicity which the Camel Trophy could generate in Australia at precisely the right time. The Trophy was to take place in March, and the Perentie announcement was expected in the summer. If Land Rover did win the contract, then the news coming on top of the Camel Trophy publicity would give the marque a powerful boost in Australia. If the contract went elsewhere, the Camel Trophy would at least demonstrate something positive about the marque.

Once again, however, the timing of the 1986 event did not marry up well with new-model launches. It was too early for the Range Rover Turbo D (to be announced in April) and for the Diesel Turbo utilities (planned for June), and so Solihull chose once again to use naturally-aspirated diesel Ninetys, which had shown up extremely well in the terrible conditions of the 1985 event in Borneo.

Among the special equipment fitted to the 14 team vehicles by SVO at Solihull were a roof rack, which carried additional lighting, Michelin XCL tyres and a Warn 8274 winch. All the vehicles were decked out in the yellow Camel livery, with the names of their crews painted on the wings; and a small fleet of One Tens was also prepared, to provide support for the crews and their vehicles and to carry the journalists covering the event.

The 2,000km route through Queensland and the Northern Territory took the participants into areas of such remote wilderness that an acclimatization run from Cairns to Cookstown in Queensland was planned to precede it. Yet despite the careful planning which had gone into the 1986

event, the main Trophy route had changed out of all recognition from the one which had been recce'd earlier. The weather had not behaved as expected, and the teams found themselves driving across rock-hard mud which had cracked in the sun, instead of through soft wet mud.

This inevitably took its toll on the vehicles. Wheels, tyres and dampers took a hammering; vehicles had to slide down steep banks into rivers with a low water level, where the plan had been for controlled descents into deeper water. By the time the convoy reached the grassland areas, the Ninetys had suffered a lot of damage. Nevertheless, the 1986 Camel Trophy was notable for the way the crews kept to the planned schedule, despite the slower progress demanded by the conditions they encountered. All the vehicles reached the finish at Darwin, except for a One Ten allocated to some journalists, which was rolled. The winners of the Australian event were declared to be the French team of Jacques Mambre and Michel Courvallet; the British team finished in a creditable ninth place.

1988 – Sulawesi

The venue chosen for the 1988 Camel Trophy was Sulawesi, one of the less well-known islands in the massive Indonesian archipelago. After training in the UK, the 12 teams flew out to Manado to join their vehicles in time for the scheduled start on March 24. The Land Rovers – One Ten Diesel Turbos this time – were equipped in much the same way as earlier Camel Trophy vehicles, with roof racks, additional lighting, snorkels, Warn winches and a full internal rollcage.

Temperatures in the high 90s and humidity to match made the first four special tasks on the northern tip of the island especially challenging. Heavy rains restricted visibility, and several vehicles had problems on the slippery narrow tracks. Bonnet-deep water on river crossings was among the hazards as the crews made their way slowly southwards, going down the trans-Sulawesi highway and then up into the mountain passes which led to the so-called Lost Coast. Progress was so difficult here that two crews, among them the British pair of Mark Day and Jim Benson, walked ahead of the convoy to clear obstacles. To get the

One Ten Diesel Turbos follow the route of a river on the 1988 Camel Trophy event in Sulawesi.

Brazil was the venue for the 1989 Camel Trophy, the last one to feature Land Rover utilities as the crew vehicles. On this occasion, they were once again One Ten Diesel Turbo models. However, utility Land Rovers would continue to be used as support vehicles on subsequent Camel Trophy events, even though the competing crews drove Discoverys.

whole convoy 54km through the mountains, 31 trees had to be felled by chain-sawing and the vehicles had to be winched through difficult sections no fewer than 16 times. Yet it was in this section that one of the more positive elements of the Camel Trophy showed up, and one which more recent events have consciously highlighted: the convoy provided assistance to local inhabitants by opening up roads which had been blocked for months by landslides and tree falls.

This ninth Camel Trophy event was won by the Turkish team for the best overall performance, but it was the British crew which won the votes of the other competitors to take home the Team Spirit Award.

1989 – Brazil
The 1989 event was to be the Camel Trophy's tenth anniversary, and so it was fitting that it should return to the Brazilian Amazon where the first event had been held in 1980. As in 1988, initial selection and training of the crews were held in Britain, and for this year there was further

training in the Canary Islands. There was training, too, for the photographers and journalists invited to cover the event, who this time were to ride in the vehicles with the crews.

This year saw Land Rover without a new product to promote, and so once again the vehicles chosen for the 14 crews were One Ten Diesel Turbos. Their equipment was as comprehensive as usual, but for 1989 it was supplemented by a split-charge electrical system with two heavy-duty batteries: repeated use of the electric winch on previous Trophy events had drained the vehicles' batteries, and this was therefore a precautionary measure.

The 1989 Trophy started at Alta Floresta on March 29 and wound its way over more than 1,300 miles of steaming tropical jungle to end in Manaus on April 4. This time, the winning team was British – a first for the event – and the Team Spirit Award went to the Belgian pair of Peter Denys and Frank Dewitte.

Ex-Camel vehicles
Some of the Land Rovers used on the Camel Trophy events in the Eighties eventually found their way onto the secondhand market, and their association with the event makes them a prized buy for enthusiasts. However, not every coil-sprung Land Rover in Camel Trophy colours has been a crew vehicle; some of them served their time as recce or support vehicles, and some enterprising individuals have even built their own Camel Trophy lookalikes out of quite ordinary Ninetys and One Tens.

Naturally, genuine Camel Trophy vehicles tend to command rather higher prices than ordinary Land Rovers of the same age, and the temptation must be there for the unscrupulous to construct fakes. Anyone who plans to buy a Land Rover described as "ex-Camel Trophy" would therefore be well-advised to make a note of its VIN number and registration number and to check its authenticity with Land Rover Ltd.

Adventure
From the very early days of Land Rover production, the vehicle has been considered an excellent expedition workhorse. The long-wheelbase variants in particular offer the right combination of space, carrying capacity and ruggedness to take those who wish to see the world for themselves anywhere a vehicle can reasonably be expected to go. Crossing deserts in Africa or exploring the snows of Iceland, a Land Rover One Ten is a reliable companion.

However, it is vital that Land Rover owners thinking of their own personal odyssey should plan as carefully as they possibly can. Things can and do go wrong on such expeditions, not least when sudden political changes leave travellers trapped in a war zone or unable to cross a formerly open border; and any vehicle taken on such a voyage should be very thoroughly prepared and in tip-top mechanical condition. There are several reputable companies which can advise on preparing for long-distance overland travel by Land Rover, and they advertise regularly in the leading 4x4 magazines.

Properly planned, voyages of this type can be a once-in-a-lifetime experience, and even more limited overland treks can prove unforgettable. With a modern coil-sprung Land Rover as their base camp, the limit for today's adventurers is the limit of their own imagination.

CHAPTER 9

Debit and credit

Buying and owning a coil-sprung Land Rover

People buy Land Rovers for all sorts of reasons, and before embarking on the ownership of a coil-sprung model you should decide exactly what you expect from it. There are so many different variations that it is all too easy to buy the wrong vehicle, become disappointed and miss out on the enjoyment which should accompany Land Rover ownership.

Choosing your Land Rover
A very large proportion of those who are looking for a coil-sprung Land Rover these days probably want little more than an alternative to a conventional car or estate car. If that is what you want, then nothing other than a Station Wagon will prove satisfactory. For higher levels of comfort and equipment, make sure it is a County Station Wagon – and do read the warnings later in this chapter about genuine and non-genuine County models. Some would-be Land Rover owners want a fine-weather fun vehicle as an alternative to an open sportscar. If that is you, the vehicle you want will be a soft-top model; and make sure the vendor knows the difference between a full soft-top (with canvas cab roof) and a truck cab with canvas tilt *before* you waste time going to see the wrong vehicle! The short-wheelbase Ninety and Defender 90 are probably the best bet in this category, but remember that the rear seats are inward-facing and do not have seat-belts on vehicles built before the 1996 model-year. (The US-model Defender 90 soft-top does have a forward-facing rear seat and proper seat-belts, however.)

Many people also buy a Land Rover for towing. In this case, it is important that you are clear about what you want to tow before buying the towing vehicle. Short-wheelbase models do tow well, but are best used with small trailers and horse boxes. For towing very long caravans, power boats and other large trailers, the greater stability of a One Ten or Defender 110 is very much preferable. It is important also to check the weight of the trailer against the recommended maximum for the vehicle. True, relatively few trailers exceed the recommended towing weights for any Land Rover, but it is advisable to check against the figures provided in Appendix A before rushing out and buying a vehicle. ,

Off the road, of course, different criteria apply. If you are buying a Land Rover to use for recreational off-roading, your best bet will be a Ninety or Defender 90, because their short wheelbases make them less likely than the 110-inch wheelbase models to catch their bellies on humps and ridges. Their shorter rear overhangs also mean that they stand less chance of catching their tails at the bottom of steep ascents or steep descents.

It should be quite obvious from Chapter 5 that a proportion of coil-sprung Land Rovers will have special-purpose bodywork. As often as not, vehicles such as fire tenders and tipper trucks are sold within specialist commercial circles for further use, but some of them do emerge onto the civilian market from time to time. Unless you have a particular wish to own such a vehicle (either to use as it was originally intended or to preserve as an

Start by deciding what you are going to use your Land Rover for. This Ninety can cope with the weight of this trailer (which contains a glider), but a One Ten would give greater stability.

interesting Land Rover in its own right), you would do well to steer clear of them; in most cases, they are simply not a practical everyday alternative to a more conventional Land Rover. Ambulance and Quadtec bodies may be suitable for conversion to vehicles such as campers, of course – but that is a decision for you to take in the light of how much effort you want to expend on the conversion. Lastly, the Land Rover 127 and Defender 130 models are, to all intents and purposes, too big for practical everyday use, regardless of the body fitted. They are best left in the commercial circles for which they were built.

Having decided on the wheelbase length and body type you want, the next stage is to choose from the variety of engines on offer. Leaving out the fuel-injected 3.9-litre petrol V8 offered only in the USA and Canada, there have been no fewer than nine since the coil-sprung Land Rovers were introduced in 1983: four-cylinder petrol types of 2.3 and 2.5 litres, four-cylinder diesels with the same two capacities, the 2.5-litre Diesel Turbo, the 200Tdi and 300Tdi intercooled turbodiesels, and the 3.5-litre V8 in two

different states of tune. In choosing from this selection, you will probably be influenced by two main factors: fuel economy and performance.

Make no mistake, fuel economy with a Land Rover is not at all the same thing as fuel economy with a small hatchback car. The most economical engines in the coil-sprung models are the 200Tdi and 300Tdi turbodiesels, and these are unlikely to give better than 30mpg on a regular basis; everyday figures of around 27-28mpg are more common. The older Diesel Turbo should manage about 24-25mpg, the 2.3-litre and 2.5-litre naturally aspirated engines slightly more. As for the petrol engines, expect figures in the low 20s (and sometimes in the high teens) for either of the four-cylinders, and be thankful if you achieve 18mpg with either version of the V8; fuel consumption can even drop below 15mpg, especially with the original four-speed LT95 transmission. Sadly, the lighter weight of the short-wheelbase models makes little appreciable difference with any of the engine options.

The most satisfying road performance, of course, comes

Bullbars are a favourite cosmetic addition to a Land Rover (although they can also perform a valuable function in certain off-road situations). However, the tyres on this One Ten County are biased towards road use and would give disappointing performance off-road. This early vehicle has been fully reconditioned by The Land Rover Centre, Huddersfield, and wears side-decals from a much later specification.

from the 134bhp version of the V8, but the second best – surprisingly for those who have never driven diesel vehicles – are the Tdi turbodiesels. The older Diesel Turbo is adequate for most purposes, as is the 2.5-litre petrol engine. The 2.3-litre petrol engine is disappointingly slow, however, and the two naturally-aspirated diesels are best suited to country lanes rather than motorways. Figures in Appendix C give more precise comparisons between different models, but it is worth remembering that most modern family hatchbacks will out-drag even a 134bhp V8 at a traffic-lights Grand Prix: Land Rovers were never intended as high-performance vehicles!

Of rather less importance in most cases is the transmission. A very few early One Tens had selectable four-wheel drive, which brings no advantages and may even deter future buyers when you come to sell the vehicle on. The four-speed Range Rover gearbox in early One Ten V8s may be unburstable but it has a very agricultural, long-travel gearchange which is not particularly nice to use. The Santana-built LT85 five-speed used in later One Tens is better, but does not have as good a change as the five-speed LT77 used in the four-cylinder models. The later LT77S in Defenders has a slightly improved change, but for a really slick and modern gearchange, the only gearbox to have is the R380 fitted to Defenders from 1994. There are no factory-supplied automatics.

Even lower down the priorities list than transmissions must come wheels and tyres – but they are an important factor when buying a used Land Rover. All the coil-sprung Land Rovers were normally supplied from the factory with dual-purpose tyres which give plenty of 'bite' in soft ground and a reasonable standard of roadholding and comfort on the road. County Station Wagons usually came with the more road-biased tyres also fitted to Range Rovers, which still give a formidable amount of grip in off-road conditions together with a slightly softer and less noisy ride. Any difference from these 'standard' specifications has implications of which you should be aware.

Firstly, specialist off-road tyres generally have a more aggressive tread pattern than dual-purpose tyres. They may still qualify as dual-purpose tyres suitable for road use, but they are likely to be much noisier on the road (ask yourself why you can always hear a military Land Rover coming along a Tarmac road before you can see it!) and they may have lower standards of road grip. One of the favourite off-road tyres used on Land Rovers, for example, is positively frightening in hard driving on the road. Conversely, tyres which are more heavily biased towards road use (and which again may still qualify as dual-purpose types) are likely to be quieter but to give disappointing traction off the road – even on such undemanding surfaces as wet grass.

Secondly, many Land Rover owners insist on fitting wheels and tyres which are wider than standard, primarily to give their vehicles a more aggressive appearance. Worth remembering is that wider tyres do not automatically give better off-road traction (the tyre may 'float' instead of digging into the surface), and may well give inferior roadholding to the standard size. Without power-assisted steering, they are also likely to make parking a chore.

Vetting a Land Rover for sale

Once you have settled on the type of Land Rover which best suits your needs, you are going to start looking at examples offered for sale. These will come up most cheaply in private hands, will be rather more expensive from a 4x4 specialist (but may come with some form of reassuring guarantee) and will be most expensive of all at a Land Rover franchised dealership. You are most unlikely to find vehicles more than about five years old at a franchised dealership, by the way.

The most obvious problems on a used Land Rover are likely to be those visible on the **body**. Land Rovers get used hard and their Birmabright alloy outer panels are vulnerable to minor damage; using a knee to close a door, for example, often leaves a shallow dent. Most minor damage will be readily visible, and it is up to you how much you are prepared to tolerate. Remember, though, that the larger replacement body panels are not cheap, and that the later one-piece doors must be replaced as a unit because they cannot be reskinned. Worth particular examination is the base of the windscreen pillar on each side, which can rust quite badly just above the scuttle area and is awkward to repair neatly.

The next stage is to examine the interior. There are various different types of seats, the most comfortable being the cloth-covered County (or de luxe) type. These also wear rather better than the PVC-upholstered seats used on commercial and less expensive models. Really badly damaged seats may be replaced before a vehicle is sold, but few vendors bother to replace door trims, and damage on these can be a useful indicator of how well (or otherwise) a Land Rover has been maintained.

The **chassis** deserves a careful examination, as it can carry evidence both of major accident damage which has been repaired and of hard use in a vehicle which has been carefully prepared for sale. The tough black paint finish on these chassis does not normally allow rust to get a hold, so if rust is present there is usually a good reason. Look for evidence of accident damage which has been repaired (weld seams, plating and creases in the metal are the obvious guides), and check whether the vehicle has been used in a quarry (small stones bombarding the underside can chip the paint away) or has been used for towing boats out of the water (salt water plays havoc with steel if it finds a break in the paint covering). The crossmember underneath the gearbox may also bear the scars of heavy off-roading, and if it does, expect other evidence of this type of use to be present as well.

The **suspension, steering and axles** may also carry signs of heavy off-road use. Typical are dented front faces on the differential casings (usually the front one), bent steering rods (particularly the main drag link between the two

This very early One Ten Station Wagon – actually a pre-production vehicle registered in December 1982 – has been updated with smart eight-spoke wheels and side-steps, as well as later-specification County decals. Many enthusiasts modify their Land Rovers quite extensively to suit their needs.

wheels) and damaged damper mountings (especially the top mountings at the rear of the vehicle). Brake pipes should normally be securely anchored to the chassis frame or axle casing, and loose ones may have been snagged in heavy off-roading; it goes without saying that these need to be changed right away for safety reasons.

Other problems in these areas are mostly the result of normal wear and tear. Rust on the ball swivels inside the front wheels will damage the swivel housing seals, which then leak oil, and this in turn leads to accelerated wear of the steering components. Power-assisted steering may leak fluid, often through worn pulley bearings. Rubber suspension bushes do wear out, and worn bushes usually cause a series of clonks from underneath as the driver's foot comes on and off the throttle during gear-changing or on the overrun. Re-bushing is relatively cheap and straightforward, and there is something to be said for fitting the aftermarket polyurethane bushes, which last longer but do give a slightly firmer ride. Axle whine from the rear has usually been caused by persistent overloading, and there is

unfortunately no reliable way of telling whether the differential will carry on for thousands of miles or just a few.

Transmissions are normally fairly robust components. However, an internal seal in the four-speed LT95 on early One Tens can fail and allow all the transfer box oil to drain into the main gearbox with expensive results. For reasons which remain unclear, the transfer box on Ninetys may develop the habit of jumping out of low ratio when the accelerator is used roughly, although the same fault does not occur on One Tens. A rattle from the LT77 five-speed boxes suggests worn layshaft bearings, which are best attended to as an early priority.

Then, of course, there are the **engines**. The 3.5-litre V8's reliability and durability are legendary, but the engine does have its weak points. Rough running may be caused by carburettor problems (either tuning or more serious problems such as punctured diaphragms), and top-end rattle usually means a worn camshaft. A persistent rustling noise from the top end suggests worn rockers and rocker shafts (more expensive to replace than you might expect),

How has the vehicle you are looking at been treated by previous owners? Door trim panels are often a good guide: few early ones will have survived as well as this one.

and an irregular ticking is often caused by a sticking or worn hydraulic tappet. A V8 which is pumping clouds of blue oil smoke through its exhaust is probably suffering from blocked crankcase breathers, which are quickly and cheaply replaced, although there may be more serious causes on a very high-mileage engine.

All the four-cylinder petrol and diesel engines, and the Diesel Turbo related to them, can suffer from bore wear if their oil is not changed regularly. Leaks from the rear main bearing oil seal are also common, and the rubber camshaft drive belt will break and cause expensive internal damage unless it is changed at the appropriate intervals of 30,000 miles. These engines may also suffer from worn valve-gear, revealed by increased top-end noise and irregular running. The diesels may 'fume' (check for oil fumes from the crankcase breather) as the piston rings wear, and the Diesel Turbo may blow oil through a breather into its air filter and

block this up (check for oil stains on the filter element and for oil dripping from the filter housing).

Lastly, the two Tdi engines are pretty robust types, the earlier 200Tdi being very much noisier than the redeveloped 300Tdi. Regular oil changes are vital to both as the turbocharger is lubricated from the main oil supply and will quickly run its bearings if there is insufficient or dirty oil in the engine. The roughness of the 200Tdi can also cause oil unions and the like to come loose, and you should always investigate carefully the cause of any serious oil leaks.

Modified vehicles

A lot of coil-sprung Land Rovers offered for sale will have been modified from factory standard in one way or another. That has always been part of the Land Rover ethos: owners have modified them either to do a job of work or, since the Eighties, to reflect an image of themselves. Accessories such as bullbars, side-steps and additional lighting are either useful to you or not, and you should bargain accordingly when buying a heavily accessorized vehicle. However, it is worth giving a little guidance here on the more major modifications which some owners carry out.

The most common major modifications are to the engine and drivetrain. Lower-powered engines get swapped for V8s, V8s get uprated for more power and torque, and economical diesels get transplanted into Land Rovers with thirsty petrol engines. Early four-speed gearboxes on V8s get replaced by later five-speeds, and so on.

Obviously, the guiding principle when looking at a modification of this sort (or when thinking about one of your own) must be the quality of the work and of the replacement units used. The most common scenario is for secondhand units to be put into a Land Rover to replace worn-out items, and of course there may be no real guarantee that the secondhand items are not themselves as worn out as the ones they are replacing. It is also not uncommon to find that the implications of a modification have not been thought through and catered for: not everybody who puts a V8 into a four-cylinder Land Rover remembers to change the axles for the stronger V8 type, for

The 110-inch wheelbase was always the most popular for military models. This example was built for an overseas customer, and is equipped with a winch in its special front bumper and with a 'snorkel' for wading.

example, with comically predictable results. If in doubt about whether a vehicle really was a V8 when built, check its chassis number against the lists in Appendix B.

Some owners also go for 'foreign' engine transplants. British Perkins, Italian VM, and Japanese Mazda, Isuzu and Nissan diesel engines have all been used successfully as replacements in coil-sprung Land Rovers, and there are reputable companies in Britain who will carry out a properly-engineered conversion. In some cases, these conversions include changing the gear ratios in the transfer box to suit an engine with a lower rev limit than the original. Not surprisingly, some cheap DIY conversions neglect these finer points, and they can also be horrifyingly rough and noisy if the converter has not paid proper attention to modifying the existing engine mountings or fabricating new ones.

Many owners also upgrade the equipment levels and specification of their vehicles, and there are several reputable companies which will thoroughly rebuild an early vehicle with new parts to a later specification and thus produce an attractive hybrid. These companies are invariably quite open about what they have done, and buying direct from them need hold no fears. However, private upgrades and conversions are a minefield. Be particularly wary of assuming, for example, that County stripes on the side of a Station Wagon mean that the rest of the vehicle is up to County specification; and do not assume that Defender badges will only be found on genuine Defenders! If you are not sure about the specification a vehicle would have had when new, the identification tables in Appendix B will help to date it and Chapters 2-4 to establish its original specification. Do note, however, that

County Station Wagons have nothing in their chassis numbers to distinguish them from basic-specification Station Wagons.

Maintenance

This is not the place to repeat the maintenance advice given in the handbooks supplied with every new Land Rover, but it is the place to advise new owners to make sure they have the Owner's Maintenance Manual for their vehicle, and if not, to get one! These handbooks give sensible advice which, if followed, will keep your vehicle healthy for a very long time.

Everyone knows, or thinks he knows, that Land Rovers need almost no maintenance. Sadly, that is only half true. The fact is that a Land Rover is built strongly enough to carry on running for years and years while being systematically neglected and abused, but over a period of time a neglected vehicle will wear out much faster than one which is properly maintained.

Also worth noting under this heading is that, if you use a Land Rover off-road, you should always wash (or, even better, steam-clean) its underside afterwards. Caked mud on the underside of a vehicle can conceal all kinds of damage (such as to brake pipes or steering components) which it is better to know about at the earliest possible opportunity.

Moral support

Ownership of a Land Rover of any sort can be an essentially sociable activity. As in the more conventional classic car world, there are enthusiasts' clubs to join, all of them dedicated to helping you get the most out of your interest. Most refreshingly, the Land Rover enthusiasts' world is not disfigured by the snobbery and petty rivalries found in some parts of the classic car scene: fellow-enthusiasts are usually more interested in helping you fix a gearbox problem than in scoring concours points off you because your door handles have been too obviously rechromed!

There are so many Land Rover clubs – all over the world – that it is not practicable to list all of them here. However, if you do want to join a club, have a look in the listings in the monthly magazines dedicated to the subject. In Britain, *Land Rover Owner* and *Land Rover World* regularly publish up-to-date addresses, and in other countries the leading magazines covering the 4x4 scene can usually supply club contact details. These magazines are also the best source of information about new products and services, and will certainly lead you to your local specialists in coil-sprung Land Rovers if you have not yet discovered where they are.

Technical specifications

1) Long-wheelbase models

Note: The specifications given are for UK-market models unless noted otherwise. Dates also relate to UK models only.

a) One Ten

March 1983 to December 1984

Engines: 2,286cc (90.47mm bore x 88.9mm stroke) OHV four-cylinder petrol, with 8:1 compression ratio and Weber 32/34 DMTL twin-choke carburettor. 74bhp at 4,000rpm and 163lb.ft at 2,000rpm.

2,286cc (90.47mm bore x 88.9mm stroke) OHV four-cylinder indirect-injection diesel, with 23:1 compression ratio and CAV injection pump. 67bhp at 4,000rpm and 103lb.ft at 1,800rpm.

3,528cc (88.9mm bore x 71.1mm stroke) OHV V8 petrol, with 8.13:1 compression ratio and two Zenith-Stromberg carburettors. 114bhp at 4,000rpm and 185lb.ft at 2,500rpm.

Transmission: Four-cylinder models had LT77 five-speed main gearbox with LT230 two-speed transfer box; eight-cylinder models had LT95 four-speed main gearbox with integral two-speed transfer box. Permanent four-wheel drive with lockable centre differential standard on all models; selectable two-wheel (rear) drive optional on four-cylinder models.

Gear ratios (five-speed): 3.585:1, 2.30:1, 1.507:1, 1:1, 0.83:1, reverse 3.701:1; transfer gears 1.667:1 (High range) and 3.320:1 (Low range).

Gear ratios (four-speed): 4.069:1, 2.448:1, 1.505:1, 1:1, reverse 3.664:1; transfer gears 1.336:1 (High range) and 3.321:1 (Low range).

Front and rear axle ratios 3.54:1.

Steering, suspension and brakes: Recirculating-ball, worm-and-nut steering with 20.55:1 ratio standard; power-assisted worm-and-roller steering with 17.5:1 ratio optional. Live axles front and rear with coil springs, dual-rate at the front and hydraulic telescopic dampers; front axle located by radius arms and Panhard rod; rear axle located by radius arms, support rods and central wishbone assembly. Boge Hydromat self-energizing rear ride-levelling strut standard on County Station Wagons and optional on other models. Dual-circuit hydraulic servo-assisted brakes, with 11.8in discs at the front and 11in drums at the rear; internal expanding drum-type parking brake operating on transfer box rear output shaft. 16in wheels with 7.50 x 16 crossply tyres or (County models) 205 x 16 radial-ply tyres.

Dimensions:	Wheelbase	110 inches
	Front track	58.5 inches
	Rear track	58.5 inches
	Length	175 inches (soft-top and pick-up)
		180.3 inches (Station Wagons)
		184 inches (High-Capacity Pick-Up)
	Width	70.5 inches
	Height	80.1 inches
Weights:	3,799lb	minimum with 4-cyl petrol engine
	3,840lb	minimum with diesel engine
	3,743lb	minimum with V8 petrol engine
Payloads:	2,926lb	maximum with 4-cyl petrol engine
	2,884lb	maximum with diesel engine
	2,981lb	maximum with V8 petrol engine

(Vehicle weights with optional self-levelling suspension were slightly greater, and there was a corresponding decrease in payload.)

January 1984 to May 1984

Engines: 2,286cc diesel replaced by 2,495cc (90.47mm bore x 97mm stroke) OHV four-cylinder indirect-injection diesel with 21:1 compression ratio and DPS injection pump. 67bhp at 4,000rpm and 114lb.ft at 1,800rpm.

June 1984 to April 1985
Transmission: Selectable two-wheel drive option for four-cylinder models no longer available.

May 1985 to July 1985
Transmission: Five-speed LT85 main gearbox with LT230 transfer box replaced LT95 four-speed gearbox with integral transfer box on V8 petrol models.
   Gear ratios: 3.65:1, 2.18:1, 1.43:1, 1.1:1, 0.79:1, reverse 3.82:1; transfer gears 1.41:1 (High range) and 3.32:1 (Low range).

August 1985 to September 1986
Engines: 2,286cc petrol replaced by 2,495cc (90.47mm bore x 97mm stroke) OHV four-cylinder petrol with 8:1 compression ratio and Weber twin-choke carburettor. 83bhp at 4,000rpm and 133lb.ft at 2,000rpm.
Suspension: Anti-roll bar added to rear axle of all models with levelled suspension.

October 1986 to August 1990
Engines: 3,528cc V8 petrol engine now had two SU carburettors, 134bhp at 5,000rpm and 187lb.ft at 2,500rpm.
   Existing diesel engine supplemented by 2,495cc (90.47mm bore x 97mm stroke) OHV four-cylinder indirect-injection diesel with 21:1 compression ratio, DPS fuel pump and Garrett AiResearch T2 turbocharger. 85bhp at 4,000rpm and 150lb.ft at 1,800rpm.
Weights: Vehicle weights and payload with turbocharged diesel engine were the same as those for naturally-aspirated diesel models.

b) Defender 110
September 1990 to December 1991
Engines: 2,495cc four-cylinder turbocharged diesel engine replaced by 2,495cc (90.47mm bore x 97mm stroke) OHV four-cylinder direct-injection '200Tdi' diesel with 19.5:1 compression ratio, Bosch fuel pump and Garrett AiResearch T25 turbocharger with air-to-air intercooler. 107bhp at 3,800rpm and 188lb.ft at 1,800rpm.
Transmission: All models now had the LT77 five-speed gearbox and LT230 transfer box; gear ratios as before.
Weights and Payloads

Weights:	3,979lb	minimum with 4-cyl petrol engine
	3,981lb	minimum with V8 petrol engine
	4,030lb	minimum with naturally-aspirated diesel engine
	4,127lb	minimum with Tdi diesel engine

Payloads:	2,745lb	maximum with 4-cyl petrol engine
	2,742lb	maximum with V8 petrol engine
	2,694lb	maximum with naturally-aspirated diesel engine
	2,597lb	maximum with Tdi diesel engine

January 1992 to May 1993
Engines: 2,495cc four-cylinder petrol engine and 2,495cc four-cylinder diesel engine were no longer available.
Transmission: All models now had the LT77S five-speed gearbox; gear ratios as before.
Steering, suspension and brakes: Power-assisted steering was made standard on all models.

June 1993 to February 1994
Steering, suspension and brakes: Disc brakes replaced drum brakes on the rear axle; ventilated front disc brakes available for heavy-duty applications.

March 1994 on
Engines: 200Tdi turbodiesel replaced by 300Tdi with similar specification but 111bhp at 4,000rpm and 195lb.ft at 1,800rpm.
Transmission: LT77S gearbox replaced in all models by R380 five-speed gearbox with identical ratios.

2) Short-wheelbase models
Note: The specifications given are for UK-market models unless specified otherwise. Dates also relate to UK models only.

a) Ninety
June 1984 to April 1985
Engines: 2,286cc four-cylinder petrol and 2,495cc four-cylinder diesel; specifications as for contemporary One Ten.
Transmission: Five-speed LT77 main gearbox with two-speed LT230 transfer gearbox; specifications as for contemporary One Ten except 1.41:1 High ratio in transfer gearbox. All models had permanent four-wheel drive.
Steering, suspension and brakes: Rear ride-levelling strut not available. High Load (heavy-duty) suspension option. Front brake discs with 11.75in diameter and rear drums with 10in diameter. 6.00 x 16 crossply tyres or (County models) 205 x 16 radial-ply tyres.

Dimensions: Wheelbase   92.9 inches
Length   146.5 inches
Height   77.3 inches   (pick-up)
77.4 inches   (soft-top)
77.6 inches   (hardtop and Station Wagon)

Weights and Payloads for Ninety (to May '85)
Weights: 3,540lb   minimum with 4-cyl petrol engine
3,622lb   minimum with diesel engine
Payloads: 1,750lb   maximum with 4-cyl petrol engine
1,669lb   maximum with diesel engine

Weights and Payloads for Ninety (2) (May '85–July '85)
Weight: 3,532lb   minimum with V8 petrol engine
Payload: 1,759lb   maximum with V8 petrol engine
(High Load suspension added 59lb to vehicle weights and permitted a payload increase of 271lb.)

May 1985 to July 1985
Engines: Four-cylinder petrol and diesel types supplemented by 3,528cc V8 petrol engine; specifications as for contemporary One Ten.
Transmission: 3,528cc V8 petrol models had LT85 five-speed main gearbox with two-speed LT230 transfer gearbox. Specifications as for contemporary One Ten.

August 1985 to September 1986
Engines: 2,286cc petrol engine replaced by 2,495cc petrol engine; specifications as for contemporary One Ten.

October 1986 to August 1990
Engines: 3,528cc V8 petrol engine now uprated to 134bhp, as for contemporary 110. 2,495cc Diesel Turbo added as fourth engine option; specifications as for contemporary One Ten.

b) Defender 90
September 1990 to December 1991
Engines: 2,495cc four-cylinder turbocharged diesel engine replaced by '200Tdi' intercooled turbodiesel. Specifications as for contemporary Defender 110.
Transmission: LT77 five-speed gearbox and LT230 transfer box now standardized on all models, including V8s; gear ratios as before.

Weights and Payloads for Defender 90
Weights: 3,607lb   minimum with 4-cyl petrol engine
3,587lb   minimum with V8 petrol engine
3,651lb   minimum with naturally-aspirated diesel engine
3,734lb   minimum with Tdi diesel engine
Payloads: 1,684lb   maximum with 4-cyl petrol engine
1,704lb   maximum with V8 petrol engine
1,640lb   maximum with naturally-aspirated diesel engine
1,556lb   maximum with Tdi diesel engine

January 1992 to May 1993
Engines: 2,495cc four-cylinder petrol engine and 2,495cc four-cylinder diesel engine no longer available.
Transmission: LT77S five-speed gearbox standardized; gear ratios as before.
Steering, suspension and brakes: Power-assisted steering standard on all models.

June 1993 to February 1994
Steering, suspension and brakes: Disc brakes replaced drum brakes on the rear axle.

March 1994 on
Engines: 200Tdi turbodiesel replaced by 300Tdi with similar specification but 111bhp at 4,000rpm and 195lb.ft at 1,800rpm.
Transmission: LT77S gearbox replaced in all models by R380 five-speed gearbox with identical ratios.

3) Extended-wheelbase commercial models
Note: The specifications given are for UK-market models unless noted otherwise. Dates also relate to UK models only.

a) One Ten Crew Cab models
December 1983 to June 1985
Specifications generally as for contemporary One Ten models, but:
Dimensions: Wheelbase   127 inches
Length   198 inches
Weights: 4,167lb   minimum with V8 petrol engine
4,222lb   minimum with 4-cyl petrol engine
4,244lb   minimum with diesel engine

Payloads: 2,480lb maximum with diesel engine
2,524lb maximum with 4-cyl petrol engine
2,557lb maximum with V8 petrol engine
(The unladen weight of vehicles with levelled rear suspension increased by 22lb, and the payload decreased by 198lb.)

b) One Two Seven models
July 1985 to August 1990
Basic specification unchanged from One Ten Crew Cab models; detail specification generally similar to contemporary One Ten models.

c) Defender 130 models
September 1990 on
Basic specification unchanged from One Two Seven models; detail specification generally similar to contemporary Defender 110 models.

4) Australian-built models: brief specifications
a) One Ten Heavy-Duty ('120')
Engine: Isuzu 4BD1 3,856cc (102mm x 118mm) OHV four-cylinder direct-injection diesel, with 17:1 compression ratio. 97bhp at 3,200rpm and 188lb.ft at 1,900rpm.
Transmission: 1985 models have LT95A four-speed main gearbox with integral two-speed transfer box; 1986 and later models have LT85 five-speed main gearbox with LT230 two-speed transfer box.
Steering, suspension and brakes: No power-assisted steering option. No self-levelling rear suspension option.

Dimensions: Wheelbase 119.6 inches
Length 181.1 inches

b) One Ten Heavy-Duty 6x6
Engines: 3,528cc V8 petrol with 134bhp; 3,856cc Isuzu 4BD1 diesel with 97bhp; 3,856cc Isuzu 4BD1T turbocharged diesel with 115bhp at 3,000rpm and 231lb.ft at 2,200rpm.

Dimensions: Wheelbase 119.6 inches
Front track 66.8 inches
Rear track 66.8 inches
Length 240.7 inches
Width 88.5 inches
Height 102.4 inches

(All dimensions relate to the military ambulance model.)

Vehicle identification and production figures

Vehicle identification

All the coil-sprung Land Rovers have standardized VIN (Vehicle Identification Number) codes. A typical VIN would be SALLDHMV7A123456. The first 11 digits identify aspects of the vehicle's build specification, as shown in the table below. The last six digits are its serial number. Serial numbers began with 100001 for Solihull-built vehicles and 500001 for CKD types, but in May 1986 Land Rover incorporated all models (including Range Rovers) into a common numbering sequence. The first number in the new sequence was 261902. There was a second change in December 1990, when Defenders were once again allocated their own chassis number sequences, these starting with 700001 (Defender 90), 800001 (all CKD Defenders), and 900001 (Defender 110).

Although it is not possible to determine the build-date of a vehicle very accurately by its chassis number, the following serial numbers provided by Land Rover give an approximate guide:

184732	March 1983	First One Ten
208595	January 1984	
213333	June 1984	First Ninety
229956	January 1985	Ninety
230001	January 1985	One Ten
241937	August 1985	First One Ten with 2.5 petrol engine
256479	January 1986	One Ten
256593	January 1986	Ninety
270456	October 1986	First Ninety Diesel Turbo
281194	January 1987	
314041	January 1988	Ninety
314369	January 1988	One Ten
358393	January 1989	One Ten
358791	January 1989	Ninety
421115	January 1990	One Ten
423950	January 1990	Ninety
465686	September 1990	First Defender 110
465692	September 1990	First Defender 90
700312	January 1991	Defender 90
900380	January 1991	Defender 110
906580	January 1992	Defender 110
925366	January 1993	Defender 110
930494	January 1994	Defender 110

MANUFACTURER	MARQUE	MODEL RANGE	WHEELBASE	BODY TYPE	ENGINE	STEERING AND GEARBOX	MODEL-YEAR	ASSEMBLY LOCATION
SA = Rover Group	L= Land Rover	LD = Stage 2 Land Rover	H = 110in	A = Truck Cab, Soft-top or Hardtop	B = Diesel Turbo	1 = RHD 4-speed manual	A = 1983-1984	A = Solihull
			K = 127in	B = SWB Station Wagon	C = 2.5-litre diesel	2 = LHD 4-speed manual	B = 1985-1987	F = Overseas, from CKD
			R = 110in	E = 2-door Crew cab	D = 2.5-litre petrol	7 = RHD 5-speed manual	E = 1988	
			S = 110in (military)	F = 4-door Crew cab	F = Tdi turbodiesel	8 = LHD 5-speed manual	F = 1989	
			V= 92.9in	H = HCPU	G = 2.3-litre diesel		G = 1990	
				M = LWB Station Wagon	H = 2.3-litre petrol		H = 1991	
					M = 3.9-litre V8 (injection)		J = 1992	
					V = 3.5-litre V8 (carburettor)		K = 1993	
					Y = 2-litre T16 petrol		L = 1994	
					Z = 3.9-litre Isuzu diesel		M = 1995	
							N = 1996	

Production figures

Over the years, Land Rover have issued two different sets of annual figures: one set for actual production and the other one for sales. The sales of Land Rovers in any one calendar-year may be either more or less than the production figures: less if a drop in market demand resulted in over-production, and more if unsold vehicles from the previous year were sold in the new year. Both sets of figures are given here for comparison; in each case, they relate to calendar-year, not to model-year.

Year	Production total	Sales total
1983	28,412	28,586
1984	25,663	25,562
1985	23,772	31,046

Year	Production total	Sales total
1986	19,195	22,026
1987	20,475	20,686
1988	22,229	22,515
1989	22,738	23,088
1990	21,363	20,583
1991	18,906	18,500
1992	17,651	16,500
1993	17,590	19,375
1994	22,265	21,091
1995	26,670	26,847

APPENDIX C

Road performance figures for coil-sprung Land Rovers

Full road performance tests of the coil-sprung Land Rovers are something of a rarity. The conventional car magazines test only those models at the top end of the range which can be seen as viable alternatives to car-derived estates, and the specialist press concentrates on the vehicles' off-road ability and does not test on-road performance figures. Here, though, are some sample figures taken from leading British and US magazines.

	One Ten Stn Wgn 114bhp V8 4-speed	Ninety Stn Wgn 114bhp V8 5-speed	Ninety Stn Wgn Dsl Turbo 5-speed	One Ten Stn Wgn 134bhp V8 5-speed	Defender 90 NAS soft-top 182bhp V8 5-speed
Max speed (mph)	78.8	83.5	76	84	86
Acceleration (sec)					
0-30 mph	-	3.9	5.3	4.4	3.1
0-40mph	-	6.3	8.7	7.0	4.7
0-50mph	-	9.6	14.2	10.4	6.9
0-60mph	16.4	14.2	22.3	15.1	10.2
0-70mph	-	21.7	43.9	22.7	14.4
0-80mph	-	37.9	-	38.6	22.5
Standing ¼-mile (sec)	-	20.0	22.1	19.8	17.6
Acceleration (5th/4th)					
10-30mph	-	- / -	12.3/ -	14.3/21.4	- / -
20-40mph	-	10.5/14.8	9.5/13.1	11.7/17.8	- / -
30-50mph	10.9	10.2/15.9	10.7/13.7	11.1/17.5	- /15.1
40-60mph	-	11.2/17.7	14.2/18.8	12.1/20.1	- / -
50-70mph	19.5	15.1/23.6	- /35.5	15.5/28.4	- /20.7
60-80mph	-	- /10.2	- / -	23.9/49.8	- / -
Overall mpg	-	14.3	18	13.4	14*
Typical mpg	-	15.9	16-23	12.1-17.4	-
Kerb weight	3,942lb (1,788kg)	3,534lb (1,603kg)	3,763lb (1,707kg)	4,404lb (2,002kg)	3,880lb (1,760kg)
Source	*Motor* March 10, 1984	*Motor* May 17, 1986	*Autocar* March 25, 1987	*Autocar* Dec 9, 1987	*Car and Driver* Feb 1994

*US gallons. Equates to 16.8mpg Imperial.